10 KEYS TO CLIMB

EVEREST

BY PAT AMENT

(Illustrated by the author)

ISBN: 0-9648606-5-1

Dedicated to Robin, Cody, and Maren

Don't stand around, Corchiss,
the wind will get you every time

CONTENTS

PINNACLES OF THE FIRMAMENT

I journey in imagination to a corner of the world, a far land the high reaches of which are Everest. There is a small team of climbers, a band of friends. No other climbers are to be found, or are expected, among this mountain's icy, soaring realms. Only these valorous few are here, three… perhaps four… individuals. They are unknown to the world. They are like a little colony of artists who live richly in bitter poverty. They are on the mountain, and also in the world, for the rewards of beauty. They expect no fame, should they stand on the summit. They are drawn by the grandeur, by adventure, and toward things that best are described as spiritual. Everest tests their knowledge of anatomy and their intuition as to theories of light and values of color. Their minds are on the sculpture, as it were. Certain faces, certain expressions of the mountain, gaze downward at their camp. Everest, with all its movement and energy, hides. The climbers lose a sense of where the elbows and shoulders of the slopes are. The mountain's shapes present themselves somewhat as clouds that move, rise, lighten, and grow darker, the hundreds of reliefs, their strength, their nakedness, seen between mists and storms.

Tom Hornbein once signed a copy of his *Everest, the West Ridge*, "For Pat Ament, a fellow wanderer among the heights, a poet of the peaks and precipices and pinnacles of the firmament and of the soul." Hornbein is one of the heroes of Everest. He was a hero around Boulder, Colorado, in the 1940's, a pioneer of rock climbs on the imposing and overhanging sides of the Third Flatiron. His words, in the above inscription to me, are "luxuriance amid drought," to use language of writer David Craig (*Landmarks*, p. 185). In Hornbein's reference to "pinnacles of the firmament and of the soul," there is beauty. There is testimony of the importance of a climber's spirit. He speaks of the inner world of climbing. We all are climbers, if you think about it, and what lies at the heart of us is of more value than most outward, superficial indications that we manifest of how we are alive. Hornbein's own soul resides in a slight, inconsequential-looking body (with an impish demeanor), yet he proves to be the stature and caliber of Everest. He would not immediately convey the image of one who has forged a way to the summit of the highest mountain.

We are featureless, ultimately, as wind blows across our shapes and blows our appearances and voices into so many variations. Mountains and people are illusions of space and light. As we pass through the mirrors and fog of life, the haze of such a brief experience as mortality, what we hold to, as solace, are semblances—memories and hope, and the interactions of our spirits. A mountain, like life, discloses something of the being a climber is at his or her core.

As life moves by, as its edges close around us, or as the hours are hacked away, as it sometimes seems, we are burned, scraped, taught, softened, solidified, honed, and humbled. We contemplate the terrors of extinction. Amid storms and dust of a day, there sometimes is the nourishment of a peace, a joy, a light, something we feel, a meaning…. There are moments where even the hardened individual stands above his martyrdom and looks out at the resplendent sea of the world. There are the endless peaks and mountains of creation. In afternoon, the light is subdued, gorgeous, and without want. Independent moments of a supreme worth stand alone, apart from the blood-stained ambiguity and chaos of the world.

Reduced to basic geometry, Everest's rocks set up strong diagonals in space. Its landscapes obey principles of the still life—combined with the magic power of the pyramid. "Still life"—an interesting paired-opposite. There is something timeless, huge, unconquerable, and immovable about Everest, yet it is the most unstable place that one can imagine. It shifts, it falls, and its plays of light are ever changing. It does not define clearly its form or basic structures. To climb such a mountain, and there is only one such mountain, or attempt to climb it, is a slow, hollowing-out of one's surer feelings, and then left in the soul is a more accidental, misty, late hang of existence. Such a tranquility, if I am to compare it to kinds that I have felt in my own experience, is removed from jet engines, TV evangelists, and the thought that people are entering the country with suitcase atom bombs. Somewhere among pines at sunset, or alone in a cool, quiet of morning, perhaps with a friend on sunlit rock, or in some near illumination on a mountain of the Himalaya, are strongholds of our lives.

In the stillness of our souls, we are made aware of the shaly outcrops that we crampon upward over. We sense a climb, the movements, the shapes of rock that we twist upward between, our hands on rope, ice-axes, and holds. Rocks, mountains, become shadows of the sentience of our souls, and long after we have lost the desire for icy wind and snow to cut into our faces we are able to have their burlesques and lofty themes within. We climb up through faces of thought and through dreams and feel precarious, new expressions of rock or mountain… and ourselves. On the slopes of Everest, upward through its open secrets, the effort is to fight off those parts of our minds that are habituated to unconsciousness (or to ordinary consciousness). To save ourselves, we throw our eyes and minds at the folly of danger and beauty. Everest is steep and high. It does not lessen in scope, as do we when we fail to grow to the measure. To move upward is a challenge—whether on Everest or just in marriage, say. The heavy world holds us lower down, and we move slow in the airless height with pain in our legs and stress in our chests. We worship the loneliness up there, and that view. We believe in the brightness and not so much in the climbing.

I speak as though an Everest veteran. For the length of this book, I must permit myself—and you must permit me—to imagine it is so.

The Everest climber comes back to the regular world, returns home, and then in his manner, built into him, is a bearing, a small shiver, something fixed, as though he never will cease to shake in the dark air-space of a tent. Those who succeed at Everest are left alone in some way. In a moment when their attention strays, they stare upward. They keep, as a sacred possession, what they do not have and never could have.... In other words, it is theirs, even if it is not, and it is not... even if, for an instant at some high ridge, or on the summit, it was. Their minds and bodies continue to move toward a graceful, unprotected place of the soul that is Everest.

I cannot think of one who has said it better than Hornbein. At the end of his Everest book, he writes, "There was a hint of fear, not for our lives, but of a vast unknown which pressed in upon us. A fleeting feeling of disappointment—that after all those dreams and questions this was only a mountaintop—gave way to the suspicion that maybe there was something more, something beyond the three-dimensional form of the moment. If only it could be perceived." A few pages later, "Even now wind and falling snow would have obliterated most signs of our having been there." (*Everest, the West Ridge, abridged*, p. 135 and p. 141)

The greatness of what he had done was ephemeral, private, and—as he said—did not make him greater—in an ultimate sense—than anyone in God's eyes. Everest, like God, is no respecter of persons. I happen upon Hornbein's voice often in my mind. It "strays into my silence," to use language of poet Reg Saner (*Four-Cornered Falcon*, p. 278). I feel a certain caprice, in that Hornbein, so small in size, went there, to Everest, and to the top. He would take note of my tone, how simply I say the words that he climbed it. Is it not a somewhat benign, however very tremendous, idea that one should climb the highest mountain of them all? In a small, majestic culmination of light, Everest is the most logical of all mountains.

The "still life" of Everest has its paradox and comedy. It is difficult, I think, for a climber to have a positively balanced thought. How does one linger, for example, at "This is the most real thing that I have done" when such a thought must fight for space alongside the "What part of me will have to be amputated" thought? Somewhere between the two extremes is a route, the one I imagine Hornbein took when he simply walked up among those stars, snow, and winds. He went to look for, I would guess, or at least he probably met, what poet laureate Howard Nemerov calls "the poetic quality of strangeness." Nemerov describes poetry as "whatever the marvelous power of language causes to remain hidden from us." (*Figures of Thought*, p. 34) One might apply words of this sort to climbing. It is whatever the marvelous power of a mountain (or rock) causes to remain hidden to us.

In hope that I might get at "what I know until I try to tell you," I will say that the imposing figure of Everest first renders to us light and space and then the excitement of a strangeness… told to us in part by patron saints who died or disappeared up there and who lie in wait. They are frozen in the slopes. We study the deep, high realms, the feel, the way the mountain keeps its distance as it draws us in. With a consciousness that seems to ever awaken, we look outward, upward, into the light of the world. Viewed by some as essentially a random fact is this mountain, Everest, with its ambiences of adventure and nearness of death. As readers, or writers, we find in such strata experience that is original and searching. With much thought, we prepare the way for ourselves. We go there. Everest expresses our desolation and our longing.

The snow and ice are steeped in sadnesses as silent as death, and it will be equally easy to lose ourselves in their happiness, the cliffs, sky, and clouds. We desire to find what we know we will keep hidden from ourselves.

Bishop to Queen Three, Norton

1. REALIZE IT'S JUST NOT AN IMPORTANT THING TO DO

"No army has ever attacked Everest, and probably none ever will, for the good and obvious reason that the venture would be a useless one. That, when all is said and done, is the very essence of mountaineering. That it is, by materialistic standards, useless… that it is one of those rare and precious human activities that man performs for their own sake, and for that alone."

--James Ramsey Ullman (*Kingdom of Adventure*, p.29)

If there is one thing to be said about Everest, it is high. So is to fly in a jetliner. Does that make it a worthy end? To reach a great height in a jet is a somewhat simple procedure, not much to think about, it seems. To climb Everest, on the other hand, is a project of great danger, effort, and expense and to which climbers attach the utmost importance. They seek direct contact with Everest's slopes each year and, in some cases, make themselves admirably suited to the rigors that the mountain requires. High-keyed spirits, who hold a certain level of skill in their hands, take steps through snow. With suspicious glances and somewhat cadaverous faces, they go up and place themselves among the famous structures of ice, snow, and ridge. Each Everest climber has a vision of the mountain that might better be described in his or her own poetry. It is difficult and personal. Human figures are swallowed up in the limitless expanse of sky and promontory and lose themselves somewhat among the progressively diminishing hexagons of rock and snow. Sovereign in its command of space, Everest seems no less than, and ever more, an object of mystic composition, full and monumental.

According to an image I have of Everest, the climber seems often about to vaporize… or is painted in moonlight—the effect of an almost yellow light in photographs that I recall. There also is the dark manner of Everest, its mysteries that shepherd individuals deeper, upward, into danger and more complexly into those visions we refer to as personal. Everest is snow, wind, and cold, a world the spatial organization of which the reasoning intelligence discovers is difficult to follow. A climber ascends, descends, and traverses…. References are lost. Yet the strangeness somehow is a match of the climber's inner existence. The mountain is the color of places a climber knows, and doesn't know, and finds sacred, and can't quite get to, as with truth and with dreams.

A book about Everest, one would think, should begin at a drawing table, or desk, and work its way perhaps in the direction of the summit. In the case of this book, we shall say that the summit of the mountain has been reached. We at least feel some kind of desire, in our collective minds, to have had the experience of the summit.

It suddenly is the descent that is before us. Do we have time to get down to the next camp before dark, before we will be required to attempt a dangerous, cold bivouac out in the open on a slope where we will be exposed to the fury and severity of the elements? Questions of less importance also dog us in their silly but mysterious way. Did we take all the pictures we wanted? Will we be able to provide proof that we were here? If other climbers are on the ridge below, they will be able to testify of our success. Most, however, will be too oxygen deprived to notice much of anything beyond the steps before them that their feet must next take.

I see David Breashears. There he is. He stares into an I-MAX camera. The film to be made from his footage will earn $68,000,000 its first year. I wonder what his cut will be. It is none of my concern, but he does not seem the type to spend the time to bargain a good deal. For him, I imagine, the reward is to be here on the mountain and to have the film equipment with which to be creative (in a large format way). Where would the producers of that movie be without him? They will capitalize on his willingness to climb and on his unconcern that he be, as he should, one of the principal shareholders. He will go on, and he will get by. He will write a book, and he will tour. Everest possesses his soul, and he possesses riches of it that are greater than coin.

David could offer to us some important information about the descent, how long it will take.… I wonder if he sends messages mind to mind, to his companions? He is a reflective soul, more so than he gives people reason to believe. I do not know if he would read Shakespeare in a tent, as did Everest pioneer George Leigh-Mallory to T. Howard Somervell high on the mountain. David would not likely have in his mind so much of the cosmic wonder and odd extravagances of digression that now fill me. As your companion on the mountain, I will, in quiet, psychic style, share with you a few paradoxes of life, as they come to me. It will help us to pass the descent. There is little light left. Our minds are fortunately joined. They are connected to the atmosphere and to the footing, and we have an ability to communicate as we stroll downward. I will be able to speak to you, without speaking. If you will hear, without hearing, you will be unharmed. It will be better for you if you do not fight what I have to say. We must expend as little effort as possible. We must conserve strength.

Your thought now might be of a thermos of warm drink, or new oxygen bottle. It makes for more thirst to think how good it will be to drink something. The soreness of my throat increases when I imagine what is needed to soothe it. Each breath is more laborious when I ponder fresh oxygen, so I place in my mind other thoughts—some of which will reach you in the silent, mind-to-mind way.

What is Everest? A long walk? A world of diminishing returns? Its very beginnings are auspicious, to be blessed by a Lama, or touched by his silver prayer wheel, to see fine weather ahead, all during the miles of approach, a sense of error as is the case when the war ahead appears fun…. The pygmies of our minds, the reporters, begin to talk of exclusive rights. The steps get harder, our minds more silent, as we move closer to our demise. The very names of climbers serve as subtle warning. For example: John de Vere Hazard (of the 1924 Mallory-Irvine expedition), or Steve Strain (of a North Face expedition, 1987). As Everest first "recommends itself unto our gentle senses" (*Macbeth*, Act 1, Scene 60), we say confidently (in the silent way inside) the words of climber Rene Desmaison, "Cold and exhaustion are mere incidentals on the road to victory." (*Total Alpinism*, p. 97) The cocky, impertinent sound of such a remark can be replaced with a sense of its wryness. Desmaison certainly was experienced enough to keep obliviousness and pride in perspective. The true Desmaison says,

"Mountains bring me something more profound than danger, more lasting than the kick of a nasty moment survived. No one who does not climb (an awkward double-negative) can appreciate the cold beauty of the Alps in winter, the exhilaration as dawn comes up over the Chamonix Aiguilles, the glory of sun and wind and snow." (*Total Alpinism*, p. 97)

With visions of mere incidentals, along the road to victory, we are greeted by wind that howls with hurricane ferocity at base camp. An appalling, cheerless, first night is spent below the mountain proper. We shut every embrasure of our soon to be wind-shredded tents. We sit and shiver in what mountaineer Geoffrey Winthrop Young called "reluctant seclusion." (*Armchair Mountaineer*, p. 355) We have visions of the death bivouac, when in August 1935, Max Sedlmayer and Karl Mehringer became chilled fixtures of the Eiger.

Then, as the sun warms and glorifies the earth once more, and there is less wind, to look upward is to see a maze of crevasses. Bodies live there. It was

Don Whillans who said with his trademark sardonic brevity, "The mountains give, and the mountains take." We contemplate the way icefalls and glaciers move. We hope on this trip that one of us is not taken. We hope also that those crevasses and ice slopes do not, for the moment, give up any of their dead.

The way I see it, Linkwie,
after this adventure
we'll be friends forever

When Chomolungma, the name given the mountain by Tibetans, was renamed Everest, in 1865, after the Surveyor-General of India, Sir George Everest, it was about fifty-six years before actual climbers (or at least any of which we know) would go up onto the mountain and map what might be learned of themselves. Lone individuals would be put together in teams to survey the high, forbidding secrets of the Himalaya and how such secrets might compare to the high, forbidding secrets of those individuals who were sent. When Mallory and cohorts explored the way to Everest, they first were concerned with how to keep themselves alive, fed, and warm. Those priorities have not changed to this day. By necessity, by cold and lack of air, by the ways of wind and struggle, the human body is stressed. The mountain works on the nerves of a man. The summit must remain a secondary consideration. Death probably occurs most often when the summit becomes the first order of business.

Mallory, in his visits to Everest (beginning in 1921), took note of the effects of altitude and learned a few things about acclimatization. The laboratory of the loftiest of mountains must have been, for him, and undoubtedly is for any climber, half real and half fabulous. It was a fact that he and his companions could not refer to Everest as an obliging and courteous host. Beyond survival and logistics, however, were structures of snow, statues of ice, and grandeurs of terror that lay in wait, the grimly positioned snow and ice flanks, eerie mists, a dreamlike appearing and disappearing of the mountain, its blackish shoulders and disquieting plumes of snow that indicate formidable wind…. Gales roar across the upper reaches. The mountain is not only dreamlike but in fact a dream, and a climber is one of the mysteries, a stranger, in it.

An ascent of Everest is not to master the impossible. Clearly it is not impossible to climb the mountain. We have done it. It has been attained many times, despite the fact that… so small a matter as a boot fitting a shade too tight may endanger a man's foot and involve an entire party in retreat (to paraphrase Mallory). Climbers do not approach Everest in order to embrace the most profound level of technical achievement. That will be found in rock climbing and other more technical mountains. The reason we are here is more along the lines of a respect for Everest, that we should gain insight into it, with the assumption that we will gain some modest look at ourselves also, from inside out, as it were, or upsidedown, and some parts of us may prove accessible only on Everest.

Because Everest is not unattainable, the reason we are up here must be for the purpose of going to one of the strongest, strangest, most beautiful environments in the world. We are here for the sake of private, inner adventure (despite the mental communications that unite us). We are here because we are attracted to the experience of climbing. We press upward, or downward, connected by joy to life, in a place where mere incidentals have the potential to swallow us, and sometimes we appear almost to let them. No one in his right mind will get a big head. On Everest, after all, you move, usually, along the weakest lines of the mountain. If you think you are great, the mountain has other sides you will never do. I cannot recall a single Everest climber who ever boasted about his (or her) ascent. I have heard a few boast about how badly they failed. Many have been the boastful types, the self-centered ones, before their ascent. Something changes. They are new-made when they return.

I would imagine Breashears would say he climbed Everest for the conquest of a personal goal, or because he loves to be in the mountains. After he hurt his back in a fall rock climbing, he gravitated toward mountaineering. Before he knew it, he was at the top of Everest. Time flies, and we look over our lives and see who we were and how things were destined to unfold for us. Were David's goals ever selfish? It proves most often with David Breashears, at least so far as I know him, that he has a flair for altruism as opposed to pettiness. He usually assists or saves someone along the way of his climbs, and this has been true for him on Everest. Or he helps people find in themselves the spirit to go on—whether up or down.

For me, Everest is a kind of primordial foolishness—the way cave-men once played at the edge of volcanoes, and thought they might jump in (or so we conjecture). I go to Everest because I know its wind will blow some of the stale sanity off me. Some of the dirt too will be blown away. I go to face myself. I am a far greater opponent to myself than most mountains or rocks ever could be to me. I don't need a mountain to render myself mentally disabled. The rarefied air, every step a supreme effort of will, the prodigious exertion of one step after the exhausting completion of the previous step…, but in the foregoing case I refer to the stairs in my home. My interest in Everest is that I stand an outside chance of having dinner with the Abominable Snowman. Almost any climber might fit that description, after weeks on a mountain. Life is not unlike Everest. It always has seemed for me a bit uphill.

Some who go to Everest say it is to climb, others to explore and feel the rigors and dangers of the Himalaya. To say, "I have been to the top of the world," is a phrase adequate to the task of many things. It describes, if you will, the "sheer joy" (to use George Leigh-Mallory's words) of no more than being on Everest's slopes. Who would not feel 'at the top of the world' to arrive, simply, at Thyangboche and the temple in a certain light of a brilliant day? That would be sheer joy, with snow on the hillsides, to feel and have been brought by the long approach to within touch of the exhilaration of the greatest mountains.

**Is it slippery
up there, Goodwick?**

James Ramsey Ullman points out an interesting fact, or "fascinating aspect," that the highest elevation on earth almost exactly coincides with the highest elevation at which man, without artificial aids, is able to live. Inherent in this fact is, it seems, some kind of divine implication that… Everest was meant to be climbed. The substratosphere's cold, the bitter, rarefied heights, ice-sheathed minds, perception dulled, judgment gone, will and body atrophied, the dispiriting hugeness of the mountain, the labor of lungs, ice walls that crumble suddenly and undermine one's keenness, heights guarded by paralyzing wind, the upper pyramid of the mountain unapproachable except for a few days here or there of practical climbing weather, and even then in the grip of death, and a companion's gloomy little words of encouragement…. To think about it is enough to freeze a climber where he stands. Yet we are at the top, the top of a world, that place where we draw the line, above which no man can venture or live. We are at the top because we have made this the highest, most important place in our minds, one of the watch-points of our mortal kingdom, a brief but terrifyingly glorious fortification atop which we have made it our destiny to stand. Through centuries of war, romance, and adventure, this is the point that gazes down over all.

We are the kind who appreciate life at its most intense and beautiful. This is our gift, our ability, to go places that make us feel and feel to an extreme. We could not feel here at all, were we not able to feel in every rock and lower place and soul we have met and will meet. In everything, and everyone, there is an essence….

Confronted with the descent from the summit, we wonder what chance there is that we will get back alive. We hope to tell about our experience. We hope to share with our friends a few of Everest's mysteries. We must move lower, where there is air. We have reached a tired, and hence a dangerous, condition of the mind. Fear becomes a "meaningless concept," as described by

Rene Desmaison in his account of finishing his winter ascent of the Walker Spur. He says, "We no longer felt any responsibility for ourselves; we simply existed, uncaring, in a boundless, timeless universe." (*Total Alpinism*, p. 73) We perhaps wonder how it is that we should be up here in such a plight, where wind-rate and pulse-rate compete, where we are happy and at the same time in a state of removed despair.

For some climbers, and I include myself, the high point of any ascent is the point at which the mind is most heightened. The turnaround point—where to go down becomes the right, next step—may well prove to be at the Khumbu Icefall. Who would dare to say such individuals did not go far, or did not reach high enough in their souls? Walter Bonatti wrote, "I hold that the primary quality of a living creature is courage, in whatever form." (*The Great Days*, p. 156) The key line: "courage, *in whatever form.*"

Freedom of decision is one of the prime environments necessary for a successful adventure. This is the mentality one needs, if there is to be a true chance for happiness and success. When we get worried about how important the feat is, how tied to the project we are, how committed we are to the drive and whims of others, how filled we are with the article or book that we have agreed to write, or that will be written by those who are our editors, so that we can look good and make them a lot of money, and when we think how small we are, and that our lives are held in the hands of others, and how struck we are by our own prominence in the high matters of Everest, and when we contemplate the embarrassment we will feel should we fail… any weight the mountain might carry in our souls diminishes. Only when things don't matter too much do they gain the power to be the most beautiful and mystical. Thus I envision a team of climbers a few in number, a little colony of artists who live in bitter poverty and do not do what they do for fame. They are there rather because of the beauty of a place, a place as organic as art.

I hope these thoughts will become oxygen to you, my fellow climbers, as your tanks become empty, but back to the top of the mountain. Let's think of the good that we have brought to the world by our being here. We have done something to improve at least ourselves, and that will help the world. It is a first step. Do we imagine ourselves heroes? Does this place we stand matter to us, or are we concerned with how people will take note of us? I want to be a hero to my daughter. I have long since given up on the climbing world. What I think we need to say to ourselves, as we slog in some broad way upward, or downward, is that Everest, in the context of the fame of it and the public awe, is not an important thing to do. There is no other way I can think of to say what is, in fact, a complex and difficult notion. In the light of real fatigue, but also in light of those mystic ends, those things that *are* important can, for some people, be found on Everest. These slopes can breathe to one at least some sense of what they mean.

Do you dream? Isn't it interesting, when our unconscious minds process events, scenes, and materials of the world? In dreams, we rarely see ourselves in positions to receive praise. The conscious mind, however, entertains visions and schemes, and we are a three-ringed circus of self-praise if the praise of others does not attend. When we are "well" in our minds, success appears to surround—at least potentially and peripherally. We like success. Without it, we would feel at a serious disadvantage in a competitive, money-driven world. We are human, so we forgive ourselves for our vanity. We must forgive ourselves for almost everything. Somewhere within, we know the goal is to move more toward the dream aspect and away from the superficial patterns of the carnal and pedestrian world. The key is to get to that place where we are alone enough to look into ourselves and see where we have been and see places toward which we are en route. We must do something to give ourselves that small, sacred shiver. We must not ask, "How will it look if we fail?"—a worry of too many climbers and people of any kind. Another climber asks in his silent mind,

"How will it look if I worry about how it will look if I fail?" He is doing the same thing, but in a more intellectual way. So I have to be careful in my words here, that I do not put on an appearance.

The key is to genuinely be concerned about others but not be governed by their opinions. We only can live our own individual lives. Life is made better as we absorb the love and good of others, but the shiver is our own. We remind ourselves, out of respect for the scriptures, that all things are given to us by God, and thus contradictions of thought flow around us on Everest like a sun that scorches us in frigid air. Part of the definition of integrity is respectful independence. Let that thought blow into your brain.

Part of the integrity of an ascent is to keep things in some kind of light. Shall I precede the word "light" with "spiritual?" This might not seem a very specific or correct kind of language, but I will put everything I have said so far in the context of an example.

In 1996, Beck Weathers was in extreme danger, his hands frostbitten beyond saving, after he had spent a night lying outside, alone, on Everest. Written off as dead, he arose like a zombie and, by some blessing, found his way downward to a tent. Later, after being helped to one of the lower camps, he watched in agreement as the first chance at a helicopter rescue was given to the more severely injured Makalu Gau. Beck's participation, however small, in this decision, was heroic. His gentle compliance and spirit in general were placed before the world to observe. An ascent of Everest suddenly glanced away into relative unimportance by comparison. (*Everest, Mountain Without Mercy*, pp. 178-179, 187, 236-238)

Weathers made a poignant statement later that what he had been looking for on Everest he now knew he'd had all along, in his life and his family.

Gatchel is checking the windometer

2. BRING LOTS OF LADDERS

"Climbing is all about facing the unknown, and the outcome should remain uncertain until the end…. It is only when climbers part company with the fixed ropes that proper climbing begins."
—Doug Scott (*Himalayan Climber*, p. 35)

Everest would be a more serious matter, were you to have to climb into and out of its crevasses. The trend is to walk over the top of them with ladders. Certainly to engage the Khumbu icefall, ladders greatly reduce the time exposed to the dangers. Groaning, collapsing blocks of ice are better negotiated quickly. Anyway, it takes a long time to climb down into and out of a crevasse. A good, old-fashioned, house ladder stretched across the top of the deep cavern makes for less hardship and a good few steps of exhilaration (even a photo of excellent content downward past two boots through the rungs of the ladder to infinity). One wonders if climbers become gnomes when they disappear down there. It is, or it was at one time, Tibetan legend that demons live inside the earth—as a geologist by the name of Heron discovered in 1921 when he dug holes and infuriated the locals. I digress.

The way breath makes visible its shape on a cold day, so is the body shaped to types of moments and kinds of equipment. The heavier the pack, the more stooped one becomes. He or she is more comfortable, however, when the provisions of the pack are spilled out at a camp and found to be bounteous. The fine, poetic line is to carry as much as possible without wearing yourself away with too much.

Whatever the equipment we use, it molds us. Artificial oxygen itself is equipment. A certain puckish grin may forever be built into Tom Hornbein's smile, as a result of too much oxygen.

If there is a challenge that cannot be overcome with the right equipment, we the world do not know of it. The challenge of Everest seems to decrease slightly each year as technology increases. There also are individuals, as in rock climbng, who keep ability rather wildly on the rise. Yet today's age (which always can be called so for only a moment at most) seems one of technology and equipment as much as athleticism or art. The gear in some cases, as always, supplants ability, while in another number of cases the equipment magnifies the ever more profound physical will and inclinations of the newest elite.

There are those who altogether dispense with certain types of apparatus critical to the success of the majority of people. The solo rock climber dispenses with a rope, for example. Done away with, on Everest with a few climbers, is oxygen-aided climbing (other than what oxygen they hold in their bodies and find up here on the mountain).

It is not a bad thing to be oxygen-aided… or to have the best possible equipment. Tweed jackets (with wind-proof shells) were the standard once and, I imagine, not all that helpful in fighting off the wind's rage or the imminent doom of the high mountain environment. We need not return to that. It is possible, however, to think about those people, the early pioneers of mountaineering, the experience of their adventures, how they climbed up steep, hard snow toward the silence of the Himalaya with so little technology and even less security. Great mountaineer Reinhold Messner says about Mallory and Irvine that they used equipment (and clothing) "...with which I would not climb the Matterhorn." (*Free Spirit*) As a kid, I had only Kletterschue to walk up steep snow and ice slopes of a certain Colorado mountain of my youth. Depending on how hard the snow was, there were a few moments in which I stared at a hundred foot, two-second slide to the sharp boulders below. How easy that snow would have been with crampons or an ice axe. The new ice tools allow one the privilege of ascending almost anywhere on an icy mountain. Climbers sometimes even ascend rock now with their ice tools, simply to keep from breaking the rhythm during those mixed climbs which turn from ice to rock and back again. It would be harder to go from bouldering to ice, with only chalk and shoes.

Advance, from a technological point of view, is appropriate. Yet the dangerous extreme, and what we hope to avoid, is an era in which people attempt to work out their very salvation with fear, trembling, engineering, and tools. My mind wanders ahead to some brave new world. I imagine timed-release oxygen pellets upholstered into tent floors, each climber with his own Gamow bag. The Nepalese government might as well go ahead and build an escalator system up through the Khumbu icefall. The framework of the escalator would have to be of a certain flexible plastic....

Climbing objectives aren't worth much if one of the vanguard ideas is to organize, conquer and destroy...at the cost of beauty, friendship, honesty, and whatever else that might be spiritual, artistic, wholesome, or good. I wonder if climbers will evolve altogether away from the use of supplemental oxygen on Everest (except perhaps to have it on hand in the event of a medical emergency). I mean, why not use scuba gear and an oxygen tank to see how long you can stay underwater before you must come up for air?

To digress again, I have wondered in my slightly out-of-shape, hard-pumping heart of hearts, and excuse me if I reveal a lack of scientific understanding (it's actually a shortage of oxygen for the moment), why, and I say why, with all the wind up on Everest's ridges, air should be in short supply? Isn't wind air? Why not just open the mouth and fill up?

The issue of oxygen is, to me, a critical one. Doesn't it dramatically alleviate the problems of altitude and acclimatization? To not use it keeps alive the full challenge of the mountain, and it makes defeat more acceptable. I wonder when the step was made from the high jump to the pole vault. At some point, some person was determined to jump higher than all the rest. He added the use of a pole. Walt Unsworth, in his book about Everest, says, "When it comes to a question of self-esteem, Man is a pretty sneaky sort of creature. If he sees a game in which the rules consistently damage his vanity, he changes the rules." (*Everest*, p. 225)

People were smart enough in time (after much observing and pondering) to realize a difference in having jumped so high with the help of a pole. The two endeavors were made separate events. With Everest, there are oxygen ascents and much rarer, non-oxygen ascents. There are tweed jacket ascents and Gamow bag ascents.

If this book inspires you to attempt Everest without oxygen, and the result is your death, I apologize ahead of time. I do not believe in disclaimers. I do not believe in saying, "The author is not responsible for anything he says in this book," or "Climbing is dangerous, and the editors do not stand behind a word of the text…just in case you get killed and want to sue." Almost any climber should be able to discern, by the time he or she is up here on the wind-rich slopes of Everest, whether or not he (or she) is able to breathe…without supplemental oxygen.

Making good
progress toward
the
final
ridge

In 1978, Reinhold Messner and Peter Habeler, who five years earlier had climbed the north wall of the Eiger in ten hours, showed Everest to be climbable without high-altitude porters or use of artificial oxygen. Was this the first ascent of Everest?

Messner's August 1980 solo of Everest in three days, without oxygen, was an incredible achievement, even if his motives are said to have been clogged by what a coup the ascent would be. There is an outside chance others had soloed Everest, including for example Mick Burke in 1975—after which he soon disappeared on the mountain. Yasuo Kato finished up the North Ridge alone in May 1980, but Messner wanted to start his solo lower, from the foot of the North Col and go up and return entirely alone, without pre-established camps, prepared caches, or a support team. It could not be argued very convincingly that Messner was in it for the cheap thrill, in light of the fact that he was willing to pay $50,000 dollars imposed upon him by the Chinese. To play in the spindrift, one must be somewhat of a spendthrift. He just operated on what air was up there, little that it is. He opened his mouth and filled up. Who will question his motives?

Hermann Buhl is thought to have invented this notion of a pure, self-contained ascent without oxygen. Buhl called it "Westalpenstil." That sounds, if you say it right, remarkably like, "Rest, stop, and stand still." Buhl ascended Broad Peak (8,047 meters) in such a way in 1957 (according to Kurt Diemberger, *Summits And Secrets*, p. 337). This was not a pure, truly unsupported solo. I. F. Mummery certainly also had attempted Nanga Parbat in 1895 in a self-contained way without oxygen and perished very high on the mountain. Buhl, in his book *Lonely Challenge*, writes, "Mummery, that great mountaineer…." George Mallory thought along the lines of no oxygen in the mid-1920's. Mallory wanted to climb Everest without oxygen. He saw oxygen as a detriment to the human spirit. Now that Ang Rita Sherpa, for example, has made many ascents of Everest, all without oxygen, it is easy to appreciate the vision of Mallory and Buhl. In 1999, Babu Chhiri, without bottled oxygen, made his eighth ascent of the mountain. He stayed at the summit a record twenty-one hours.

If there is a question why climbers would use oxygen, then it is equally easy to ask why a climber would go without oxygen. If the climber who uses oxygen is merely trying to ensure success, and perhaps hopes to prove something to himself or someone else, might the climber who forgoes oxygen also wish to prove something? The question asked of those who carry bottled oxygen, "Why do they use it," philosophically should apply to those who don't. There must be a deeper issue here at hand, and I intend to dig with my snow shovel and prove to myself and others that I can succeed and find it. I am destined to end up in a cave for the night. The real essential here might be that no amount of oxygen will get you to the top if, by virtue of some element of your mind and spirit, you have no business on the mountain in the first place.

I found Mephisto, he's looking weak

A thought was just given clearance and has arrived, welcome or not. For the sake of traversing away from questions I cannot answer, I will share this new thought and, for a moment, put an end to whatever tone with which I was stumbling about in the previous paragraph. Namely, there is plenty of brain damage in lower worlds.

At one time, there were many mountains that seemed secretly to hope for a climber. Now the spirit of those high places feels a bit laconic, not exactly talkative… in a spiritual way… except perhaps to send some storm to punish and impede in a small measure the eerie, often ugly, apocalypse of climbers that has made itself so dramatic in the most recent three or four decades of the 20th Century.

Pucelle, I believe we have
lost the route

3.   HAVE YAKS AND SHERPAS CARRY ALL THE HEAVY STUFF.

"What will not be pure enough for one person will be acceptable for another."
—Royal Robbins (*Advanced Rockcraft*, p. 83)

Let's backtrack a few steps. I would like to stand on this ridge for the length of time it takes to breathe several breaths. We need to rest. Let's think. I am not satisfied with what we have found up here at this moment. I am not ready to descend, to complete the expedition, to squelch the high, to face myself in a lower world…. There is Breashears again. He is near the end of another ascent of the mountain. How does he do it? He is honest. This honesty is something we wish to have. I want to have an Everest level of honesty about what I have achieved. I want to realize who I am in relationship to the mountain. British climbing legend Joe Brown mentions in his book a fellow who seconds a rock climb, falls off nearly every move, and when he gets to the top says, "That was nice, I wish I had led it." (*The Hard Years*, p. 18)

I am bothered by the notion that I think I have conquered Everest. I do not believe such a feeling, such a vainglory. Do I anticipate praise? Do I hope recognition will be pointed in my direction? Will I allow it and wallow there and use such fame to my advantage in earning money? There could not be anything wrong with that, could there? Somehow it bothers me to think about it. There are many reasons Mallory is a hero, but one reason is that he disappeared on the mountain and avoided all the press.

I don't imagine Breashears over-indulges in self-admiration. He would not exploit his fame. He is driven foremost, I will conjecture, by a need to perform his duties, to carry them out as exactly as he is able, and... to live life well. I am bothered by the fact that so much of my gear has been lugged up to base-camp and other places of this mountain by yaks, porters, and Sherpas. How is it that I should get so much credit for the climb? Somehow I want to see a Sherpa as more than a dolly with a brain. When and if I bring a yak along it will be only to have it there. I have no other reason to use a yak than to listen to it bellow or see or smell it. I have no desire to make it carry a thing, unless it clearly could communicate to me that it wanted to. Yaks have proven to be excellent luggage carriers, although it is the sad story of one expedition that a yak was loaded so top-heavy it fell off a cliff.

In 1977, Gerry Roach wrote, "Everest can be climbed by a much smaller team using few if any Sherpas." Roach adds, "Someday I would like to return to Everest with a team and tackle the mountain head on, like the rock back home. Maybe it won't work, but to find out is the reason for going." (*Everybody's Everest, Quest*, 77) The critical phrase: "...like the rock back home." Gerry has made a vital comparison between a Himalayan mountain, in all its power and cold, and the joyful, sunlit rock of a climber's "backyard." His backyard has been lovely pine forests filled with sandstone, above Boulder, Colorado, and warm, starlit nights of Eldorado....

There is a glaze to Everest just now, its slopes like frosting. It seems that we have a taste for the effects of weather and wind. We cleave to the subtle, magical light of the broad, expansive, flats of snow and rock of Everest. There are passageways to which we are drawn, upward through the mountain's facades of stone.

How much drudgery are we willing to inflict upon others to make ourselves light? In rock climbing, the feeling is to move upward without being weighted down by equipment, body, or mind.... The weight I inflicted on people as a young climber was the concern some felt for me, my being somewhat mad…then. I was a dead weight a few times and dangled at the end of a rope, but that was during those periods of development (after which I became more often the one who lifted and held the weight).

Another random thought has blown down from a ridge to me. Such thoughts, though of little use, provide relief and break things up. Along the lines of how equipment affects the appearance of people, one might muse that a yak is a Sherpa re-formed by the labors of years. There are, after all, with the Sherpas, those questions of reincarnation. But off that, a better thought: yaks represent the irrational aspect of the art. They bear some of the haunting, abstract facial casts of a mountain itself. As the trail toward Everest moves above all the more typical vestiges of worldly charm, yaks lumber up great, oblong reliefs with their loads. Somewhat stiff and lifeless seeming, their eyes mirror our personal destinies or our longings that are hidden. To patrons of Everest, there must exist some hideous
sense of the weakness of man.
To walk in a line with those
yaks, we are no worse, and
hardly better.

**Emergency
tent pole
replacement**

Let us begin to rationalize. No one achieves much of anything alone. The hardest work of any achievement usually is left to someone else. Climbing is life. You want to do it all yourself, but you know you cannot. When others help, you feel diminished. When it becomes clear that their absence would mean your utter annihilation instead of success, you are inspired by them. When you contemplate to what degree they will have to be credited for the success, you feel cheated a little, at first, and for a moment you deny that they made so much of a contribution. Then soon you call upon a certain honesty. You are realistic and at least somewhat humble and acknowledge them and that they are probably, in most cases, better climbers than you. If they fail, however, to perform their duties exactly right, you wrest the job from them with noticeable force. You think, for an oxygen-deprived moment, again, that you will do it all yourself. Then almost immediately you give it back to them, for you are tired.

I was told in my earliest days as a climber that I should never take anything into the mountains that I was not willing to carry out. Yaks, Sherpas, and helicopter drops have made it possible to have lots of the modern conveniences of home. Since Everest is far away, many do not mind if it becomes a landfill. George Carlin points out that "sanitary landfill" is a euphemism for "the dump." Conservation, ecology, protecting the environment… are not philosophies that have been wildly heeded on Everest. We see writings that discuss the surge in garbage, oxygen canisters, plastic, glass, batteries, tin…. We are told of the increasing presence of erosion, human waste, graffiti, litter, and bodies—all of which lie unburied about the slopes. We are told that "the environment hangs in a delicate balance." The truth of the matter is that the environment is likely to survive. It has been through millions of years and will be there long after we are gone, as Carlin proposes in one of his comic dialogues.

It is the spirit of the experience that hangs in a delicate balance. The success of an expedition might not be judged by whether someone reaches the summit. It should be judged by whether or not the time spent on the mountain upgraded the mountain's beauty—rather than degrading it. A mountain's beauty is "upgraded" by virtue of the spirit that is infused into its slopes by those who pass near it. We are told in scripture to multiply and replenish the earth. The key word is "replenish," which means to give back. If we hope to draw into our spirits the beauty of Everest, we must return to it whatever is, or should be, some of the beauty that hangs along the edges of our souls. The inner feeling and ideas of those who visit the area are what is left there, and sometimes those attitudes and spirits are every bit as much garbage as piles of discarded oxygen bottles. The criteria for success should be measured by whether the experience has been one of integrity, of pristine awareness, and love for one another and for the mountains. I would prefer to see a team sacrifice the summit than argue about who the summit team should be. I would perfer to see a team waste forty thousand dollars than make the noise of another canister dropped into the rocks of an afternoon's silence.

Many of the Sherpa climbers probably notice right away that they are better, stronger climbers than those whose loads they carry. Their test is not the mountain, rather a test of humility… to continue the act of the inferior, or the slave, and not embarrass the masters. Many of the locals of the Everest region of the world have broken out and have shown they are able to summit as easily as the next person. That was the beautiful thing about Hillary and Tenzing's second ascent of Everest, that Tenzing Norgay, Sherpa, should prove the equal of the other best man for the job at that moment.

Perhaps your thoughts cling now to the words, "second ascent." We know that Mallory (and perhaps also his partner Irvine) pushed well over 8000m into the death zone in 1924. Since no one has yet proven that the summit was not reached by them after they were sighted by Noel Odell so high on the mountain, it is no sin to give the two early pioneers some kind of spiritual benefit of the doubt that the ascent was successful. Mallory was determined. He had been part of two previous expeditions to the mountain that had failed. Sir Francis Younghusband wrote, of Mallory, "In his mind must have been present the idea of all or nothing. Of the two alternatives, to turn back a third time, or to die, the latter was for Mallory probably the easier." (*The Epic of Mount Everest*, Chapter XXV) Mallory wrote in a letter to his wife, during the third and final expedition, "It is almost unthinkable with this plan that I shan't get to the top; I can't see myself coming down defeated." (E. F. Norton, Mallory's letters, as cited in *Everest*, p. 110)

Mallory spoke of his determination to Tom Longstaff: "We are going to sail to the top this time and God with us—or stamp to the top with our teeth in the wind." (*Everest*, p. 111) Longstaff wrote in a letter to a friend, "Nothing could have stopped these two with the goal well in their grasp at long last." (*Everest*, p. 134) Even the great mountaineer Geoffrey Winthrop Young believed the accident happened on the way down, after the ascent had been made. (*Everest*, p. 134) A modern climbing great, Stephen Venables, says in a *High Magazine* article of 1999, "Mallory could conceivably have reached the summit, with or without oxygen, with or without Irvine." Venables cites his own ascent and describes himself as an "untrained non-athlete" who succeeded without oxygen. Mallory and Irvine used oxygen, which (if it worked properly) may have given them the needed strength. How strong were they? We make a mistake when we think that Mallory and Irvine were little, wimpy, British men. They may well have been adequately acclimatized to succeed and may have been good enough on rock to figure a way up or around the Second Step. The weather for Mallory and Irvine was clear but for a brief (although possibly very serious and incapacitating) storm. Odell, their companion on the mountain, believed there was a strong probability of their success. Messner (in the above mentioned issue of *High Magazine*) feels that Mallory and Irvine did not succeed. He nevertheless calls their ascent "a masterpiece from the early days of high altitude climbing."

Whether or not Mallory and Irvine were able to achieve the final steps of Everest, it easily might be said that they "conquered" the mountain. The most prophetic of Mallory's remarks was an allusion to "unfriendly glories," beautiful summation of his death. (Letter to David Pye, *Everest*, p. 70)

The Hillary-Tenzing ascent of Everest, with the summit reached May 29, 1953, could not, I suppose, help but feel anti-climactic. In Unsworth's history of Everest, a photo of Tenzing (standing at the top) pays tribute to Mallory and Irvine by the caption, "The first *successful* ascent of the world's highest mountain." It certainly is the tendency to include in our definition of success that we return alive.

I am off track here. My point is to speak about the forces of experience that pull us in different ways. There is the upward pull of our desire. There is the downward pull of actual ability. Or the other way around. There are the great places our abilities allow us to go but for the absence of sufficient desire. There is the vision of a parade down a New York street, and there is the depressing notion that our helpers, who are to remain mostly unrewarded, have carried the main burden of the work. There is the revulsion, along with the love. There is the terrible quiet, and there is the loud, stinging, freeze of wind. We have our inner voices that would love to maintain their solitude but that are brought out somehow to rage in the silence that never goes away, the silence and the fury whose voices are too close always or too far away to be ignored. Yet we ignore them. We certainly can hear the Sherpa mind, the humility, the concern, the respect for gods of the mountain, and for the mountain, as opposed to our slower, western respect…. But that is a generalization, for which I hope I may be forgiven. That is a stereotype, and I know many "westerners" who respect the mountains, and their gods, very much. A mind is full of error and also fights with a host of truths, and a climber sometimes does not know which direction s/he is headed--up, down, or sideways. The only hope is to have all the regard in the world for the smallest brick of stone, or ice, of Everest.

We are told by scientists that whatever is in time travels in at least two directions simultaneously, into the future as well as into the past. Thus the pull of the summit and the attraction of home…. In like fashion occurs the struggle of the fundamentally schizophrenic climber divided in two by what is sane in him. Thus we do need help in our causes. We need hand and foot warmers. We need special clothing. We need amazing amounts of food. We need oxygen, fixed ropes…. We need Yaks and Sherpas to carry us. Huge blocks of marble were carried for and to Michelangelo and Rodan. Then they claimed the victory with their chisels. This is the way it is in mountaineering, unless you are Mallory or Messner—or other few who have, it might be said, climbed Everest, in the true, alone sense of the word. No, Mallory was not alone. He had Irvine. Yet in some ways, he was alone. I believe I am able to say this without a doubt.

To get a big idea as to our achievements slights those around us who do much of the ground work. My mother did much of the ground work in my life. For years she changed diapers, washed clothes, took me to school, fed me, put me to bed, woke me up, and made sure I didn't burn up the house. And that was after I had graduated from college. She suffered as she allowed me the freedom to become a rock climber, to be driven somewhat psychotic by all the perils of youth…. She stands with me on the summit, and is—without question—the stronger climber of the two of us.

Breashears acted as Sherpa for a number of expeditions before he was recognized as team-leader material. He was team-leader material from the start. His spirit was bursting at the seams. I remember stories about him carrying loads of gear for others. He went up and down the mountain, from one camp to another, back and forth enough times to have climbed the mountain. It seems a kind of justice that he should be one of those to do Everest, and without oxygen (apart from natural sources). I like his sense of how we depend on each other in all aspects of our lives. He admits he stands on the shoulders of those who have helped him.

I love my mother. One thing she taught me is that the things of most beauty in the world are worth suffering for. We must be what it takes to have those things that are beautiful, and to achieve any such things requires a lot of help. Any involvement with others in a world that keeps us usually so alone is part of the greatness of Everest or of any other of life's masterpieces of experience.

O.K., Jacopo, I think I'm getting
the hang of these crampons

Nice save, Bozzetti.
Let's get you back up here,
and look where you step next time.

4. REALIZE FAR WORSE CLIMBERS THAN YOU HAVE DONE IT.

"I used to go out looking for epics at one time. When the weather was bad, the snow coming down and a wind rattling the windows I'd thrust out of the door and set off into the Carneddau, seeking the white-out, the wind-howled slopes streamered with snow. I would brace my shoulders and pump fists and head pugilistic against the gusts until I was up there on the whale-roll of the great ridges with the snow-pall obliterating all stored sense of place."
—Jim Perrin (*High Magazine*, 1986)

"What's your next climb? Everest?" or "So when are you going to climb Everest?" (and be a real man) etc. Questions such as this are often asked of devoted rock climbers who do not have the desire to be mountaineers. It is about the same as to ask a gymnast when he is going to run a marathon. The question does not fit and instantly becomes irritating. Like Mallory, who coined the quick (but perhaps subtly mystical) answer to why a man climbs a mountain, "Because it is there," I have had my own reply to those who could not separate in their minds the slopes of Everest and the cracks of Yosemite: "My grandmother could do Everest." This has not meant that I lacked generosity in my assessment of the difficulties of Everest.

Most grandmothers could not do Everest. They would probably only make it to the South Col.

It's a good thing Everest
is not too steep, or I
wouldn't be able to walk down
with this snow blindness

The people who have tromped up Everest, guided or stepping along in the footsteps of a superior climber, form an amazing consortium. It has been proven that skill is not the prime factor so much as money, desire, and weather. I say this without the slightest desire to belittle Everest or anyone who is rich.

One of the classic men of distinguished valor of mountaineering has been Sir Edmund Hillary. We imagine his heavenward look of striving, of struggle and Gothic spirit. In the depths of his essence (or is it our essence?), he performed life before everyone's eyes, brought us back to life, led us free and away from the more "proper" destiny of boredom or intransience. He found the way. Ever since Hillary and Tenzing, and long before, Everest has been a standard by which men have chosen to gauge themselves. It is the highest mountain and, from its summit, has a beautiful, full-circle view of the earth. Beauty and danger combine, as an environment. If it were the fourth highest, but the same mountain, would the view seem as good? If there were three other peaks of the same height nearby, would many give their all to suffer any of those often straightforward and sometimes monotonous slopes? However high, Everest is not yet celestial. Terrestrial, we shall believe for the moment, is good enough.

The grandeur of the Himalayas is the true reward of tromping around the cloudy, melancholia of Everest. Against a palette of blues and grays, the climber works upward. His point of view is to look from below upward—at foreboding clouds. There is breathless little more to it. But because it kills so many people, the endeavor is the focus of the world's hoards of disaster voyeurs. Because its tales are so cold, because of the mystique of its history, and because it is the highest, Everest draws the most notoriety and interest in terms of media, readers, and mountaineers. Hillary is probably a great guy, and I think those who know him would say so readily. It is not, however, the Edmund the Conqueror Hillary, the Lurch (or Jaws)-looking giant, of whom I wish to speak. Not that individual who returned to the Himalayas and built schools for the Sherpa children. It is not the man who has enjoyed worldwide fame and milked it for decades and for all it is worth, and given so many fun slide-shows around the world. I do not speak about the knighted, hero Sir Hillary, the symbol Hillary, whose signature is worth hundreds to Mike Chessler and other book sellers. It is the flesh and spirit Hillary we admire, the man who stepped onto the summit of Everest in 1953 at the same moment companion Tenzing Norgay did. That is the flag they left on top, a flag of friendship, of international fellowship, as they looked for but failed to find, astonishingly, any evidence or footprints left there thirty years before by Mallory or Irvine.

We cannot go very far without heroes to impel us. Mallory and Irvine are mine. That is not so much because they ventured so near the top. I have other, better reasons as well for my admiration. Each, I am determined to believe, had friends who were of more value to him than any mountain. Mallory and Irvine not only disappeared upward into a storm in 1924, and made their world wonder, but they did it together. We wish to imagine the full sacredness of friendship. I imagine it was enough to power Mallory beyond and above the "Second Step." I think others are troubled that he might not have been troubled by any of those steps. They forget. He had the friendship of Irvine. He had a wife who loved him.

As I consider Walt Unsworth's analysis of whether or not Mallory and Irvine made it over the difficult looking "Second Step," I contemplate the fact that Odell, the only witness, speaks about scampering up a hundred-foot rock to get in position to view them before they disappeared into mist. This little ascent of Odell's may be underestimated as a point of analysis. If he could so easily climb that rock, would Mallory have had trouble on the upper step—described almost in the same way, as a rock of about 100 feet? The altitude difference undoubtedly was a factor, but here again… is a spark of hope.

Every climber is asked if s/he wants to climb Everest. To be a climber, you will be asked as many times as there are steps along the final ridge to the summit. Our grandmothers are up there right now, at the North Col. I wonder if Hillary was asked whether or not, having done Everest, he wanted to move on now to the much more difficult Gill boulder in Eldorado?

I know Everest is my master. There has never been a question in my mind. I never could be on Everest with a thought that I should achieve the mastery. I respect what Captain John Noel wrote of Mallory in 1927, "I could notice that he was always trying to convince himself that he could beat the mountain but at the same time he seemed to show a consciousness somehow or other that the mountain held the mastery." (*The Story of Everest*)

Mallory reminds me of John Gill, because of their modesty and the isolation that they have required of their experience. Gill's humility has been a nice tact, or rather an enduring virtue, although in a quiet way he is, I believe, proud of what he climbs. No one has any reason to fault that slight "arrogance." People can (and will try to) dismiss Gill as "only a boulderer." Those who feel such a thing generally could not ascend the jungle gym of a playground without an upper belay. Those hung-up on the Everest hype, and who believe bouldering—by being small in size—is somehow less of an experience, are the typical takers of the latest mass hysteria about Everest and who provide such a rich audience for publishers. Whatever in Lucretius climbing is, it is not ONLY slogging up a snow slope in arctic cold with a modified douche bag strapped to your face.

The way I look at Everest is the way I look at any climb—even a boulder problem. I am there to feel. I put a value on my life by placing it in a beautiful terrain, and I do so safely, as humbly as possible, and with as much perception as oxygen will allow.

Today's techno-freaks will never be as unequipped as Mallory, and many of them might not end up any different. The key is to admire Mummery or Norton or Somervell or Odell or Mallory rather than surpass them. That's when the gods begin to smile on the mountain. That's when the touch of the Lama's silver prayer wheel sets in. One cannot have respect for the mountains if one does not have respect for those who have gone before. You will never equal anyone else's efforts. To think otherwise is to summon the monsoon, early. We commune with those around us, all who have gone before and perhaps those who are yet to have the experience of mortal life. In the highest light, we all are friends. That is a difficult light to reach.

Reduced to pattern and line, Everest is brilliant. The eyes of a climber render it in masses, and he becomes shy, half mystic, half hermit, as he breaks contact with the constructs of success and failure. Sun-bleached, windswept rock enters the climber. The idea of such a mountain demands the moves, upward through snow, be executed with a relative ease. Friendship, the spirit of adventure, and those beautiful things that remain hidden to us… are what require the hard-edged application of paint in the hands of a master. And then wind replaces all other traces of our strokes.

5. REALIZE FAR BETTER CLIMBERS THAN YOU HAVE FAILED AT IT.

"We must remember that the highest of mountains is capable of severity, a severity so awful and so fatal that the wiser sort of men do well to think and tremble...."

--George Leigh-Mallory (*Mount Everest:The Reconnaissance*)

Straight above, in the sky's spatial depth, the heights of Everest are hidden. The sudden, anarchic sense of one's presence among such beautiful, windy fury and bands of rock is exaggerated—for the length of a number of breaths. The process throws one outside his or her body a few moments to watch the arm of the body cut out a foothold. Even in summer, it is a winter landscape. A high place that the eye catches shimmers. The optical effect is a lacy, carved, gold polychromy of rock. Everything above is a monumental underscore of perspective, and it will take a Renaissance effort to make the next fifty yards upward. There is a peculiar rapture in the way the mind constructs space and then rejects it, then sees infinity in light. We evoke moods better than we define forms. Shadows are not absence of light, they are only a sense of things that are mysterious and strangely darker because they are more certain.

I imagine almost anyone who has climbed Everest would admit to a certain luck. To climb Everest must always be a matter of pushing one's luck. Experts speak about the small window of acclimatization, after which the physical rundown is rapid. If a block of ice, or a snow slope, collapses, you could be a great climber or a mediocre one. It won't make a difference. Even Messner fell into a crevasse near the beginning of his solo ascent. By a miracle, he was unhurt and found a way to climb out. It was not his time to die. Nor was the great English rock climber Joe Brown immune to an unsteady step on the Mustagh Tower. Brown writes,

"I was suffering from pins and needles caused by lack of oxygen. I fell through a snow cornice and only just managed to support myself on my arms. You could look straight through the hole down to the glacier 7,000 feet below." (*The Hard Years*, p. 131)

When a crevasse or cornice opens beneath the feet, a good climber will fall through with almost as much of the pull of gravity as a lesser climber, although he may catch himself. When the weather comes up, on Everest, and temperatures drop to sub-life, it becomes more and more difficult to differentiate between guide and client.

We would "conquer" anything in this world, a world rich with challenge, glory, and play, but are kept at bay by the need to rest, sleep, eat, breathe, slow down, and think… if such is possible, under the roar of wind on Everest. We cannot function long in the atmosphere of Everest, a third as much air as normal. Such weather and altitude reduce even the best climbers to mere mortals and, in some cases, fill them with the will only to lie down, be still, sleep, and be perfectly unacknowledged.

A glance across the windswept slopes of Everest jolts us with a succession of joys as well as regrets. On the good side of such confusion, we accept our portion in life—"an appearance of moral commitment mixed with a deliberate—even a flaunted—nonsophistication," to borrow language from

William Stafford (*Poet's Choice*, p. 143). On Everest there are emergences as well as emergencies of consciousness. Among climbers are refusals to think or speak alongside lunges of communication. To climb on these forbidden realms is a process of locating oneself constantly. Ridges, stones, footprints, sky, snow, rope, breath… command our allegiance—a perception that is beyond our power to analyze, in the way we would like. Yet we hazard to feel, and continue to feel, as though the images of Everest are intended to possess us, as though the various slopes, stones, and clouds are the way to get somewhere we know we must go. The influences of the mountain upon us "signal something like austere hope," as William Stafford says in a poem. We get right down to the very particles and anti-particles of experience, the elementary surfaces of snow and rock bright with electrical charges and eerie, magnetic flashes. Perpetual retrospect mingles with anticipation.

The true image of Everest is revealed at the last moment, not as we walk upward, nor as we escape gratefully down, not in a tent, bored with an hour's stillness… (just after we have prayed for relief from the roar and torment of the wind). The real memory goes into making, the intense moment of perception opens, in a small, Zhivago-esque glance at sky. A footprint uplifts us. We see in some cloud, as we feel within, a tremendous, heartfelt, and formless appreciation. At this sacred instant, we feel the sad poverty of who we must be and how we must, by necessity, view the world—in such large measure without seeing. The world is hidden in so very many ways.

What appears to be oneself meets everything that is set there to tell one something else. We spend much of our lives in a state of mystification. We sense what a complex world it is. We see by the means of a step of climbing the very obscure thing our lives should be in fact. A few of us, if we fell through a cornice would not truly be missed or even miss ourselves. Others of us worry all the way up and down the steps of life that we will not be missed. We need not worry. Most of us are ingrained in the memories of those who love us. We won't leave them, and somehow this makes dying almost practical sometimes… on Everest—a tired moment says.

Ice Pitch

There are various sources of happiness. They pull at us from many directions. Promptly they follow us, wherever we escape. Yet those happinesses do not wear oxygen. How high will we go before we have them no more? This may be a reason to climb—to see who we are without all we think we are. That's why Everest is so great and why an ascent of it could never have completion. The ascent leaves us too tired to spend much time with an answer, too tired to be sure about too much at all. We have to go down, get back to ourselves, and recover enough to remember the question, and then we hope what we found, up there, is not lost. When we meet again with ourselves, we feel something of what we felt up there on the mountain, exposed, bare, stripped of our defenses, cold in some small respect. What we have from the experience, what remains of it in our minds, is not forgotten, yet what we find on the mountain can never be at any lower elevation. What is truly on the mountain tells us we will never be back the way we were. There always will be something forlorn to the visitor to Everest.

I sometimes feel I am the weakest link on the team. So how is it that I am here? How is it that I should wear nailed boots instead of the modern kind that are so warm and so much safer? How is it that I should not by now have thrown the rest of you off? I never was cooperative, in a natural way. I have an independent spirit that has mastered me approximately as often as I have mastered it. I am not a member of the Alpine Club and never could succeed at such a thing. What is it about my thoughts that flow down the ridge now to you and into you, not voice to voice but mind to mind? There are layers of color in the surfaces of Everest which, applied one upon the other, inspire. The mountain and we are together in the painting. It takes us up and allows us to surpass all other panoramas of view, each of us a black point, a small movement in light, distant, at best ghosts of air, a vague sighting by Odell.

Guess Reinhardt stayed
a few seconds too long
on the summit

6.   REALIZE YOU HAVE ALREADY SUCCEEDED AT HARDER CLIMBS

"I believe that in its own way my individualism served the cause of human progress, since my undertakings incontrovertibly demonstrated man's innate powers of self-surpassment, which lie at the heart of every great achievement."
--Walter Bonatti (*The Great Days*, p. 156)

Through a glove, one feels the frigid metal of an ice axe. What did Mallory feel? Did introspection strain his concentration or deplete his strength? Was there an intrusion of thought into his steps, perhaps of the celebration that would take place upon his return from the mountain? Was there guilt, still, for the incredible loss of seven Sherpas before his eyes in an avalanche during his 1922 attempt of Everest? Did it affect his level of desire or endurance or interfere with his decisions? When Mallory died, did it happen quickly? Too fast for him to suffer? Did he hold Irvine on the rope for a time? Did he anguish all night, before energy ran out and he froze? Did something mystical happen during the descent, one of those tricks of mind, where—as the accident befell them—they continued to believe things were going right and that they were trudging downward safely through the snow of a ridge? It must have been a formidable exposure situation. They may have tried to survive a night out in the open, after reaching the summit in exhaustion. On the other hand, maybe things were so easy, or optimistic, that they walked almost complacently off the edge of the world.

How close were George Band and Joe Brown from disaster on Kangchenjunga in 1955? How difficult was it in 1950 on Annapurna, when Maurice Herzog and Louis Lachenal managed its first ascent? Or more recent, how was it that Jerzy Kukuczka should fall, in 1989, to his death a few hundred meters from the summit of Lhotse? Did he relax? Did he run out of all capacity to exert, yet his mind so warped as to believe success in his hands?

Let me declare my admiration for any person who has climbed, or attempted, any one of the great mountains of the Himalaya or elsewhere, with or without oxygen. Yet the hardest actual climbing on Everest could be mastered quickly perhaps by a non-climber. To express such a contradiction is to affirm something remarkable about Everest. It should be viewed as a slightly absorbing point that Everest is less technical than it is overwhelming. Such should also bear a certain warning. How easy it is, for example, to walk on corniced ground. How readily one's calm expectations of Everest collapse at the sight of the walls of a crevasse or to see thousands of tons of ice explode downward. Where will the next avalanche be? In high altitude, in strong wind, a simple step becomes difficult. The Hillary Step is highly variable and probably always somewhat technical. The Lhotse face often has lots of technical climbing (45-50 degree water ice and easy rock bands). The Khumbu icefall has tough climbing in it until the ladders are up. The North Ridge has the Second Step that most climb now with the use of a fixed Chinese ladder. One single move almost anywhere on the mountain can be dangerous. The wind becomes dangerous. Thought at half speed is dangerous. Yet it is not whether you have the ability to climb Everest that is in question. It is whether you can endure and survive its terrorist conditions, the wind and altitude of the mountain, their fantastical severity. Can you rise above a weariness of spirit, as you make for the most part mundane steps upward?

The trial of yourself becomes a ghoulish aura that sometimes hovers about the mountain, a demonic blend of maniacal fury and wishful thinking, the elements and ill winds and set-backs and mental flights of fancy…. The path leads toward hallucination, possibly a mishap, or calamity…. Such things are ever close. You hope you are not under an evil star. You do not know for sure. You are certain only that you are, by choice, one of the vaporous fictions of a mountain, its slopes spectral and supernatural.

Danger is a peculiar concept. It wasn't Everest that killed Tenzing Norgay, rather cigarettes. Ambition, I would think, kills as many climbers as does apathy. There is plenty of potential for apathy on Everest. If you take a swing at your partner, it will take six seconds for your gloved hand to arrive at his oxygen-mask-covered chin….

As with any climb, on the "rocks back home" for example, the difficulties will prove to be different than what you and the rest of the world imagine they are. This may be one of the critical joys—to discover what truly is there, as opposed to what you have thought might be there, as opposed to what photos have led you to believe is there, as opposed to what people who went there have said is there, those people who might not have known where they were at the time, or any time.

We have strayed into deep, difficult snow now, and we have begun to wander as we wonder what it is we wish to say, or think. To descend, for me, has always been to peruse thought. When I hear the statement that health is the slowest possible rate at which one can die, I think Everest is one of those long, slow, good ways to live—if you survive. You never will defeat Everest. It has no underside to expose. It is the mountain, and you are the little glitch of movement on a horizon, you with your blood-red organs inside you that depend on you to show judgment, you so small and brief in the eternal wind. The mountain does not reward you the way a difficult rock pitch does in warm spring at a normal elevation. The mountain does not recognize you for your beauty, no matter how beautiful you think the mountain is or you are.

Somehow, if the earth has a spirit, and thus a mountain has a spirit, it knows that you will, in the end, drag in the dark. You will curse the earth a few times with the same throat you cough blood up in order to praise the earth. Mountains are not fooled, you, purpling, parts of you white as milk, and others black, and the pink, red, living parts as they go slowly out of you. The wind's mouth is open for another scream at the moment you do…. As fierce as you are, as much a warrior, the silent late moment could be the last.

On a slope not far from you is a cadaver. Briefly, and from a distance, you make the acquaintance. Everest is a steady, somewhat continual fellowship with death. The person lies silent. Eyes inhale moods of the Himalaya now without the terror of the living spirit behind those eyes. The spirit of that body has stepped away, gone elsewhere to tunnel among the mysteries and images of what exists beyond. The small, shattered cliffs, the sunken ledges of Everest, blow with wreaths of cloud and snow. You are weary, stand up, rope coiled in your glove, and suddenly everything and all of you is transformed.

I think of Everest in poet Reg Saner's words,

"So just how fully into awareness dare we emerge? And at what cost? In hundreds of versions the world over, one or another mythic or semihistorical figure looks upon a humongously powerful deity and is thereby destroyed by what he or she sees. Such tales imply that there's an ultimate level of awareness so awesome and terrible you can't stand it, a blaze of revelation turning to ash the mortal who beholds it unprotected." (*Reaching Keet Seel*, p. 137)

By definition, those who die on Everest saw something. They at least saw some of what they came to look for. The end of a life might be as beautiful as it is terrible to contemplate or behold. Most of us are more superficial than the opportunities around us. It is a gift that we turn our steps and climb to some powerful outlook. T. Howard Somervell called Mallory's outlook "lofty and choice, human and loving, and in a measure divine." (*After Everest*)

It is easy to imagine Mallory's studied poise and to believe he was one of those who belong up here. I still am not certain if I belong on these slopes. Mallory must have possessed what Lionel Terray (and undoubtedly a few non-climber philosophers before him) called "man's hunger for transcendence." I'm sure Terray's phrase was based in part on once having to cut his way out of an avalanche. Using a pocket knife, it took five hours for him to chisel a passage out of that "antechamber of death," as he described it. (*Conquistadors of the Useless*) Terray called himself a "madman, for whom there is no happiness but desire." (*Conquistadors of the Useless*, p. 333) Mallory and Terray seem to have been quite different in temperament, but both were masters who forced their steps up steep snow. Each was reflective and fought not to vulgarize ideals.

Life is a simple, easy place at times. For moments on Everest it is calm and restful. What remains to be understood is how Mallory should have been such a serene man, so thoughtful, and yet in a state of almost tireless fatigue and driven by the apparition of Everest.

It might make a certain kind of person happy that Mallory brought along spaghetti in a can. This might have been considered an unfair advantage, but unfortunately, at 23,000 feet, the spaghetti froze.

Bonatti's words help us move toward something I have hoped to get at, but know may not crystallize, in this chapter: "It should not be forgotten that the value of the high mountains is that of the men who measure themselves against them: otherwise they are no more than heaps of stone." (*The Great Days*, p. 184)

Stones, for a man alone, are some of the best society on Everest. They prove themselves man's friends… in their stark and faithful counsel.

Did you remember to lace your boots, Alfordale?

7. REALIZE YOU HAVE ALREADY FAILED AT EASIER CLIMBS

"Logic asks why; but the question itself is meaningless. Only the passion and the agony are real."
—Rene Desmaison (*Total Alpinism*, p. 200)

A climber is one who has the thought he can't afford. That's why many climbing expeditions feel somewhat unfortunate that they must be made up of… climbers. Some of us, however, are more than climbers. A few of us also are artists and comedians. People laugh when they try to comprehend some of the things that I say to them in their heads. This is one of my gifts, and I am aware that it could be a long descent if the words are not right. Your fear has been that you should hear something you do not wish to hear. I am in fact a slow walker. With all the sophisticated gear and assertive clothing, I am alone… a man who would, if he could, add but a few thoughts to a strange, cold museum of climbers whose living bodies and also cadavers are scattered in and about Everest.

The mountain, apart from those cadavers (or possibly in part because of them), is at times a remarkably sedate affair. There should be nothing to press us about the summit, other than those timing issues--those windows of opportunity where we begin to adapt to elevation and when we are able to function at our best for a short time before we begin to unravel. The climb must be built around what our bodies and minds tell us about ourselves. There should be no fear, if we watch and conform our actions to the weather and to our bodies and minds and to the truth. Perhaps it is because I am snow blind, but the colors of Everest, the shapes and lines, are a poetry. There should be a great deal of play in the seriousness of such a climb. Science and organization must mingle with spirit and play. That should be the goal, but many find Everest to be only demanding—an uncomfortable confusion into which they have plunged. I apologize for that word "plunged," since it connotes falling.

In choosing a poem for a certain anthology, E. E. Cummings said, "I choose this poem in the hope that it's not only a portrait of a particular person (one erect generous whole human unique being) but a celebration of the miracle of individuality—by contrast with everything knowable and collective, common and corrupting, cowardly and truthless."

The first four lines of the poem apply to Everest as well as to anything:

> My father moved through dooms of love
> through sames of am through haves of give,
> singing each morning out of each night
> my father moved through depths of height.

Cummings adds, in the poem, "for he could feel the mountains grow" and "love is the whole and more than all."

Cummings speaks of the ghostly roots to which we long. He has told us, in few words, some message that shapes for us the light of Everest. If we are to be climbers of the realms there are to feel, then we must know something of the nature of truth… in our controlled diagonal across it. We must see the purity of every color and the grays and whites around or between "that assert the majesty of creation"—to use a line from a song by Leonard Cohen.

Based on climbs that you and I have failed at already, with excuses of course, such as that they happened when we were beginners, or just after a transplant, our rivals will argue that our success now on Everest (our very presence here) proves that the mountain is not difficult. Thus you must not climb in order to triumph over your enemies or to prove to them anything at all. They never will admit to you or to themselves that they have been triumphed over. You don't want to get a dialogue going between your mind and theirs. A more important triumph is over the icicle that has begun to form behind your mask.

Everest requires many steps, a methodical, despairing monotony. One must almost sleep at times through those steps. The whole experience is a somewhat violent dislocation. There is a great stress in being this far away from home. How is one to be at ease here? Already places and slopes have moved location slightly, and colossal slopes hang just ready to fall. There is little rockfall on Everest. It is mountain fall. Large blocks of ice, some the size of an apartment, crash down on the tenants, and the landlord laughs—an awful groan of cracking and explosions. The avalanche with your name on it already has marked your coat with a flake of snow. Rocks do fall, but you are happy for one of them—relative to a rushing freight train a city block wide.

With all the effective planning that goes into Everest, it is rather too large on any sort of human scale. Its fantastic landscapes roar with that old song set to the words of John Greenleaf Whittier, "For all sad words of tongue or pen, the saddest are these: It might have been." If the manner of work at hand is to be a success, then success can and might be defined, for example, as to exhibit warmth and humanity, to keep a good spirit however far one climbs. It will be to translate mind and being into color, line, and plane, and to include, in the pigments, acts that are uncalculatedly wise and spontaneously kind. The bare materials of Everest are not always perfectly aesthetic, but one's activities upon the mountain might almost always embody impulses that are beautiful.

We court the surreal. We court fantasy, even the irrational—of which Everest itself is a serious example. It blows and spreads its paints, its whites, and all the leading human figures of its history must revert more often than not to the nonobjective—a feeling, to which we will give the name "restraint." Indeed to stand at the top of Everest, to get close to the top, is a tenuous nobility. The glory lasts about the time frame of a photo, a sudden thrill, i.e., the urge to descend as fast as possible from an approaching cloud (or away from thoughts of companions). A sense of victory is replaced by visions of home. In a few days the next breaking story is to replace your account. A new team is poised to step onto the steep walk upward, through stupendous terrain and views that astonish.

The climber is unprepared for Everest… and remains so even to the top and back, through all his ascent upward to the mount to commune with deity and down again among the lower classes. If he (or she) brings home anything, it is this: that such little objects as people, with their molten spirits, their wrinkles, and ends, hardly register amid the huge slopes of Everest.

The desire to climb Everest should be a mysterious prompting, as opposed to a desire to organize and engage. The summit should be a place close to feeling, and a realm of higher thought. Nerves and blood should flow with a beauty of feeling. If one carries any little words in mind, up to the blowing steeps of this little molehill that we make into a mountain, into the tumultuous beauty of its latest unpredicted mood, they might be from a poem called "The Descent," by William Carlos Williams:

"NO DEFEAT is made up entirely of defeat—since / the world it opens is always a place / formerly / unsuspected."

Finger check

8. REALIZE YOU WILL NEVER BE AS GOOD AS HERMANN BUHL, AND HE NEVER DID EVEREST

"It seemed to look down with cold indifference on me, mere puny man, and howl dersion in wind-gusts."
—N.E. Odell (*The Fight for Everest*)

A mountain of such size does violence to the nature of human vision. It is difficult to have a static eye. Each of our eyes normally is in slight motion, but the agitations of altitude, wind, light, and having to filter so much experience through some type of glasses or goggles, make the motion of the eyes greater. The body, in worst cases, is deceived into thinking it is in a state of R.E.M. sleep, and dreams take place while awake. Both eyes strain to work together, in harmony.

We owe our understanding to light, its fading and intensifying, its passing, revolving, rising, the to and fro of sun…. Monochrome grays lit up by hallucinatory flashes help us to establish the relative size of objects far above and distant, or far below. In some type of normal environment, things distant appear smaller to the eye. On Everest, things grow in size—to the view of our souls—as we gaze outward from ourselves and upward at the Himalaya. By whatever story we have come to be, our eyes and senses provide for us space in wide-angle construction. Such power and panorama of sight, however, does not prevent one from seeing naively or with a blindness of soul. The capacity of Everest to create disturbing and eccentric effects is a real phenomenon. Yet beauty and a greatness of experience deeply autograph our souls. If the revolt against the weaker side of ourselves is to yield results, it will call forth from us a strength like light. We always will carry in us some of Everest's luminous darkness, the mountain's shifting viewpoints, and the phosphorescent glow of its slopes.

Sources of light are many. We see, for example, through Mallory's eyes. We appreciate the epic and mythological way in which he and Irvine pursued their dreams, how they have endured (certainly in spirit and in principle). They were in harmony with nature and attuned to life, as befit great climbers, we assume. Hermann Buhl, another great climber, was capable of powerful visions (aided at times by amphetamines). He said, for example, that he was led off Nanga Parbat by a ghost.

We feel, as we remember such people as Mallory and Buhl, that we too are capable of visions. In the linear webs of rock that hang like attitudes and that convey distance and gloom, in the tumultuous and somewhat dead atmosphere of Everest, which bears always some manner of grisly interpretation of the caprices of death, life exists in its fullness. There is plenty here to look for. In the austerity of Everest's fantastic architectures we find precursors of thought. Such beginnings, small as they feel, may be greater in value than any ends that we imagine we shall attain. The fine anticipations of the mind, the first feelings of thought, the glances into real consciousness, or the awarenesses, of which we seem almost always at the alluring fringe, are as hard to reach as the summit, yet they belong to the deeper, inner realms of Everest, and to any experience of worth. The little edges of thought move and inspire us and, I believe, are where we delve for our deeper and finest art.

Buhl may likely have made an ascent of Everest, had his path not led him off the edge of a cornice June 1957 on Chogolisa in the Karakorum. There was no ghost that day, only an angel to guide him away. Toni Hiebeler, who made the first winter ascent (with three others) of the Eiger in March of 1961, found later that he was unable to acclimatize on Everest. The doors of fate swing open and closed in the high mountains of life.

Often it is the instinct of a climber, especially the young climber, to compare him or herself to climbers who went before. To do so is an example of where sight fails. The eyes cross…. Climbers who go before are always better than climbers who come after. That is a precious, simple fact, and a climber should get used to it. Even if the gradings of climbs shoot upward past the summit of Everest, you will never be able to compare yourself to Mummery, or Buhl, or Bonatti, or Egger, or Mallory…. This is one of those great axioms of life, and nothing works very well in life as long as you fail to respect such a principle. As you begin to embrace the idea (that you can never compare yourself to those who go before), you are rewarded with a conclusion, and it is the critical one, that you must climb for your own love of it and within the arena of your own sacred, individual experience. Walter Bonatti writes, "If my experiences form part of the complex web of human vicissitude, my successes belong to me alone, and, which is rare enough nowadays, I have paid for them in person." (*The Great Days*, pp. 155-156)

As I walk up the stairs of my house, and my oxygen supply drops to critical levels, I find the life-sustaining thought that I am a kind of Mallory. Of a time when Mallory felt the strain of Everest, he wrote that he experienced "a certain lack of exuberance when going uphill." (*Mount Everest: The Reconnaissance*, Chapter XV) What beautiful understatement. Thoughts of daily life adapt themselves frequently to images of Everest. For example, I was without oxygen and had collapsed, from taking care of the baby, and could hope only to quickly die. The hour had come when my wife was to be home, and would take over, and bring much needed relief. Then suddenly the vision was gone. As I sat haggard, dazed, incapable of action, the baby asked to play yet one more game or have me tell her one more story, and threatened to scream if I did not, at which time my wife phoned and said… she would be late!

People vanish on Everest. I vanish into my study to be alone on a high ridge with my work.

I think I found Camp III, Cennino

The theme of the summit bothers us, from the moment we start upward. What is it that we intend to show ourselves--that there are inestimable dangers up here only a climber is privileged to discover? Will we gain a more just or intelligent society if we weave a way upward through and about these dangers? Perhaps Everest simply is a way to release some of the spirit that bursts from our heart's blood. The most a climber can build with, on Everest, is what he or she detects of that more subtle, beautiful nature of the world, that inner mystery of things, and of oneself, that is our blessing to never fully know.

The personal truths, the resplendent revelations of life, are all that are negotiable truly and are all that a climber should wish to bring down from the mountain—other than his or her life. The black smoke of a great, Everest cloud, a sudden, silent light, a wild cold that glimmers in the hunch and shadows of a slope…. Between the sheltered origins of our life and the inevitable end is an Everest of sort for almost every person. The mountain, for the artist, may feel like sculpture that requires the care of hands. To climb Everest would always be more to him than… the thing to do. Everest, for the imaginative soul, might mean to give up a poverty of spirit in trade for a type of spiritual action, to be born once more into life. The philosopher, I suppose, will be detached and ironical about his climb. For me, it is the mere business of growing older that inspires my soul to find something more vital, something more personal than popular decline. Everest is a climb, and since there is no reason against it, the highest climb. The natural human being will go up onto the slopes of Everest and absolve him or herself of having lived too little.

Life is for the living, yes, even if it means for the dying—as a few will die on Everest. And this is an area of tension that makes us rope together tighter. The fact is, we have been warned in very real as well as quite fictitious terms about Everest. Only when we reach the wind's wail, circa somewhere between fictitious and real, do we realize how happy or unhappy we truly are. A climb is always implicative. That is, it points us out to ourselves. The dangers are there because we are. Everest, at its best, is a vision of one's enigmatic interior, raw and bleeding, strung out on those dark bands of rock like a flayed side of beef.

A climb should be to allow all the distortion in the world to happen in heart and mind, to allow the play of one's soul and let the spirit scream from within like a carcass that seeks to return to life in a storm. White strokes of wind that highlight the ridges are faces, a transparent rendering. In each thrust of lungs and muscles, we have a dramatic, new treatment of light. We look for impulses, for masterpieces within us, the feeling, the poetic, the intarsia of our double-eyed view. A puff on the oxygen tank sounds out the next step. The direction is clear.

There is something to be said about going it alone on Everest. If you are a team's best summit hope and in a moment of lightheadedness turn around, then a lot of others must go home with you. There are miles to go, and promises to have not kept. If you go solo, you answer to yourself. If interrogated about having not made the summit, you can call what you did a reconnaissance. Yet who is so antisocial as to want to go alone? I am so lonely at times that I begin to make friends with my creditors. Another part of me remains alone, by choice. Many times, the boulderer will walk around the boulders and never climb one thing. In bouldering, one does not have to report to another soul. There is the sanctifying light of afternoon....

Everything I do now is a reconnaissance, and, as Robert Frost once said about poetry, "There are things beyond all this which I care more about, and hope we all do."

Mixel, did
you remember
to bring
the sardines?

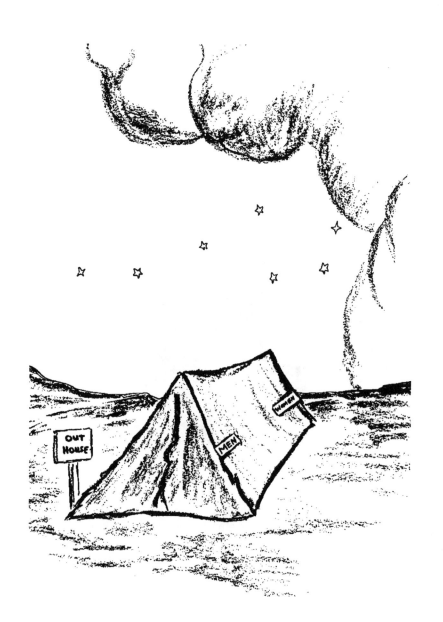

9. REALIZE THERE ARE MORE WAYS THAN ONE TO CLIMB EVEREST

"How could an impossibly complicated array of cells ever organize at all, much less seek out such a place to go?"
—David Brower (*Everest, the West Ridge*, p. 15)

Movements of light and sculptures of space. Mere incidentals along the trek upward toward that point at which we turn back.

A friend of mine, not a climber, went to Nepal and did no more than walk into the great mountains. He got a distant look at Everest, and he considered his trip very much of a success. He found it difficult to stop talking about how much fun those few days were, how much he saw, felt, and learned. His exuberance, his sensitivity to his surroundings, made me think of the disappointment so many climbers experience who fail to reach the summit of Everest. I think of how many return with only a sad countenance, sometimes having had a disastrous experience—such as the loss of fingers or toes or… a friend. It seems to be a very different perspective when we define Everest as a climb. To be in the vicinity of Everest and see the magnificent, neighboring mountains, to walk up there to any degree among such light and space and commune with that alien terrain, and a sky so shaky with storms and avalanche, should touch one's life and soul in an incredible way. To share such adventure with a friend should be entirely wonderful but for the distraction, the aesthetic myopia, the foreshortening, of that goal of the summit.

Oh what a beautiful morning,
oh what a beautiful day.
I've got a wonderful feeling
everything's going my way….

I think I am like that friend who went there with no goals. Why let something so small as Everest get in the way of something so large as the beauty of the Himalaya! Above the "Second Step," however, on the final ridge, and with the summit close at hand, there is a beauty to be found nowhere else.

There are reasons why some of us are not, in general, mountaineers. I speak of people who may be rock climbers, or may love the mountains, but are not mountaineers. Rusty Baillie once wrote about me that I would make a great Scrabble partner but that he would not want to spend many days with me in a tent. The true Everest climber must, as a kind of requirement, have an instinct, or love, for the harrowing bivouac. There must be for him some odd, cryptic pleasure in flapping tent cloth, exhaustion, strained lungs, and closeness to others.

While one type of climber exercises, marches up steep hills, and reaches points of painless bliss, as his or her endorphins kick in, another type of climber grows progressively more tired. Another climber enjoys easy walks, where there is a lot of warm, beautiful afternoon among pines, where there are silence, light, and smells of sandstone. I think of Doug Robinson's chapter heading, "Bringing Light Out of Stone," from a book with an equally gorgeous title (*A Night on the Ground, A Day in the Open*). Such phrases suggest a clarity of love for the mountains. Short, safe walks up through mild terrain sometimes have the truest of all clarity. One is able to walk up there in their own worn and winded time, a peaceful, happy fact that comes out of the light of a day. It is a blessing to be in old and friendly timber, with a child's eyes somewhat, to feel one's own presence among the pungent, resident air, limbs, and bark, and where there is lots of sun and no summit looms.

Many are better men (or women) for having not climbed Everest, in that less important way—the actual, bodily way. Many have climbed it in other ways. Many appreciate the air of where they are at present and breathe it lovingly. Some use the air to keep themselves upright, or from going mad. They breathe rich, full breaths to fight claustrophobia. Many have the seed of Everest in them, and it will blossom as it likes—and probably never too near the real and material form of that highest of pyramids.

I see, in my mind, the light of a moon across Everest some calm, warm night. What do the dead say to each other up here on these slopes when no one living is around? When everything here on Everest becomes still, and there must be such moments, there is a lovely substance. This is where my will lies. Eyes of my imagination catch the shape of a stone. I see, for an instant, a place to step, into a dream. The field breaks open for an instant like glass, or sea, toward faces of friends I love. A thought declares my love for the earth, in a moment when I do not feel angry at the earth for its cold. On Everest, I am another kind of being. I do not need all the gear. There is plenty of oxygen. Or maybe it is that I am the rock. I have joined with its spirit and see outward through its eyes at the sky and clouds and distant slopes.

Reinhold Messner, in his account of his initial, oxygenless ascent of Everest, speaks of looking up and seeing a peculiar cloud that revolved and hung over him with rainbow colors. (*Free Spirit*, p. 193). Now this gets at something important, the unusual or mystical, something beyond the face value of a scene. The first thought is that such a rainbow-filled cloud heralds bad weather. There is something more mysterious in such a view of sky and of that cloud. It is told to us simply, if we see the colors and the movement.

Chris Bonington relates an experience that took place as he descended after his climb of Everest: "I sat down every few paces, beyond thought, and just absorbed the mountains around me." (*The Everest Years*, p. 243)

These are the places where we climb Everest in fact, where we climb to its beauty and mystery, where we look upward into a rainbow cloud, where we sit and absorb the mountains....

The winds of these mountains are old. They have blown across high, barren dominions for as long as starlight has reached the earth. New stars begin to appear. Every serac that will form will fall away. The hard learning of time. Our lives unfold, still young and new in such a perspective, if we look at things right. Everest is a small part of what we are or should be. Its summit, I must say, could never be my soul's immediate joy. Its light, however, is repose. Its wind has both a body and a spirit. When I climb in a direction Everest asks me to, it suffers itself to lead me in a manner in which I will see.

Who would not feel much safer back at home, in the company of friends, with family? Yet I do not feel exactly unsafe on Everest when I have the attitude of being taught by its spirit. I am frightened by Everest, and I am not. It is cold and far away up here. It is too far from where I feel the most ease, but it does not deplete in me a knowledge that I am a good person. And this is an element of my sense of safety.

I can't climb unless I feel I am safe, that I am in touch with some feeling that I equate with love or friendship, or creativity, and sometimes God. What I feel when I condense such huge concepts is gratitude, for having been granted the gift of life. Such gratitude is found readily for me in thoughts of friends, my mother, my father, my wife, and others. I break into the madness of a beast when I slip from that line. I must stay on the route. My appreciation for their love and for their meanings brings to me the irony that they, who remain back, are my iron rod upward through danger. Only if you could understand how deeply I feel for these people would you be able to know what a lovely shock it is that I should find myself on any climb and on Everest, high up here in the foreign territory where there is trout-colored, dark stone amid slopes of snow and horrible winds that lift. I need daylight more than I need to be aloof and poised. I need to be paired with a friend more than I need to make the last push alone to a summit. I need the green cardinals of the backyard.

I feel safe that there is delicate life, that there are spirits all around… and as high up as… Everest.

A climber runs past me, with fifty times my strength. Does he actually exist? Or is he a figment of my mind? There are climbers who will go too fast to know that there are living beings. Their speed will bar some, the fast climbers, from the glory that they so cherish, if they are not careful. A few will be absorbed by their own might. A few will be among the dead, who are still alive. A memory for others will turn out to be of a sense of pride and not of the rage of wind or of the utterly living slopes that create the utterly still-eyed cadavers. One kind of climber will have defied death and moved in a straight course, and he will have added the notion of Everest to his world's goods. I will, in contrast, have played Scrabble in a tent for many days and wished I could feel warm on a rock tied to a rope with Rusty Baillie.

If you will allow me a kind of footnote in the middle of things, Scrabble is an excellent game. It may not be as deep as chess and not based as much on skill, but there is an innocence to it. The thinness of those tiny, brown tiles, the way they press against the fingers, a touch of cold to them, how you have to direct your cough away from the board to keep from blowing such light, hard-earned words off the board…. To cheat is part of the game. You knowingly misspell words, or invent words that look like real ones, and this is permissible as long as you are not caught—even then the worst is that you lose a turn. John Gill's daughter, about nine at the time, drew a fifty-five point word once and beat a certain writer who at the time was a university English student. John never would let that poor misbegotten soul forget it, that he, a writer, should be destroyed at Scrabble by a little girl.

Scrabble and chess are essential hungers of some, because of the play that they provide imagination and also because of the want that they arouse in a creative soul. The Everest climber also longs to go into such voids, such residences of the mysterious. The large, good, hidden wonders of life suffer the little players to come to them. Hopefully my discussion of such things is not entirely out of place on Everest. It too—if you care to look at it—is a game, a game of pathos, of steps and places, feet and hands, and the bones behind them, the bruised white of snow that spells out somehow the hidden and the beautiful. You sense what is inaccessible. All you need to know, however, is before you, if you have the strength to feel.

The fast climber will have proven the simple arithmetic of fitness. When he is down from the far danger, above will remain an extremely faint, barely discernible line of footprints in snow, an indication of movement. For another climber, body and spirit will have played about each other there, in light, roped together by many steps forward and downward. The decisive stroke is that life hangs by a thread, of which Everest has its many accidental and unexpected reminders. Up here on the forbidden slopes, among mere incidentals, are as many universal forces of life as anywhere, as much sadness, love, death, and exultation. There is as much faith as will be found in more "usual" worlds, although the unusual exists everywhere if we are observant. Everest is with me always, even as I cross a street… or when I am asleep. Likewise, to cross a street is with us now as we climb… Everest. As we take a breath, we feel a sense of gratitude and work out in our minds the letters for a big score.

There are many routes by which to get at a mountain, a variety of ways in which to have this mountain's kind of suffering. There are, of course, mountains of much smaller size that are, in general, as cold if not colder. On Longs Peak, in Colorado in winter, there are storms that will bury you in their ice as quickly as if you were to crawl into the meat freezer of an open bivouac on Everest. You can't light a cigarette on McKinley, I am told, for the flame will freeze in mid-strike. Almost anyone has, at one time, held his head outside a car window while speeding down a highway on a snowy, frigid day—a type of

Everest. A kid paints his face and fingers black or places a bag over his head until he begins to gasp. Who has not experienced the brief agony of "brain freeze," caused when one eats something cold too fast?

We stand as much chance,
Daumiur, of getting
to the summit
as we do seeing a Yeti

It is not with skill that I wish to climb Everest. I wish to climb it with curiosity and appreciation, with an artist's love, like my friend who walked into the mountains and never went anywhere in particular but went everywhere and saw Everest from a distance and came home happier than an Everest climber. I've had enough of skill, as an end in itself. Almost anyone can develop it. I want to be happy amid the imminent fall of things. I want to be prey to the slightly predatory nature of what is mysterious and beautiful. I want to be sunburned by the dream of life whose more diamond parts lie hidden in the rocks and in us. Climbing is a mediator between one's spirit and the earth's.

Perhaps peripheral success is what one is cut out for. Be the leader of an expedition, stay at base camp, and with the rest of the team claim victory when the climbers summit. Peripheral victory is what boxing promoters feel when their man lands a startling right. The promoter gets rich, along with the boxer. It would be interesting to see two heavyweights slug it out at Everest's summit. It would be difficult to throw more than slow-motion punches, yet it would be easier to knock someone over.

In truth, the leader who runs the show at base camp, or anyone who from the outset in no way plans to go higher than, say, the Western Cwm, might be the person to be envied in this day where so many are in a fight for high ground, where so many want to make it to the top, be heard, find the victory…. When all those competitive, hungry souls are far up the mountain, in a slow-motion boxing match for the next logistical point or best place on the final ridge at the best time, the individual whose role is peripheral is able to have to him or herself the quiet mystery of the mountain. His loneliness is not clouded by rope that needs to be paid out or toes that are near frostbitten.

Some meditate their way to the mountain, such as Buddhist monks, and in essence imagine the ascent rather than do it. There may be something to this approach. I wonder if real monks, say, on the Tibetan side, "climb" the mountain on a daily basis. They ascribe their spirits to that high place. Such becomes the means for many who never could otherwise afford an expedition. I appreciate a saying I heard recently, that living on earth is expensive but does include a free trip around the sun. I also like the statement, "Lead me not into temptation. I can find the way myself."

George Mallory and Jules Verne. Such sounds, such names, should strike the same chord in one. It was Jules Verne who coined the phrase that we are able to do anything that we imagine. We must be grateful that a notion so fantastic should reach us in this life and reach into our hearts, however stormy and childlike life requires us to be to hear it. By good fortune, we find ourselves able to implement a few points of imagination that come to press in some wild way upon our souls. Words such as "Jules," and "Verne," and "climb...," are magic. That is what climbing is about, the beauty and mystery, the inner, mystical world, the experience. Jules Verne... George Mallory.... They are the same.

We are an echo, we humans. Before we had the dangerous acknowledgment of life, which was given to us in the form of our own lives and which became manifest in affairs such as mountains and rocks, those places contained our presence. We, and I include the mountains, are what came to be when this matter we call the universe was conceived. It was created first in spirit, the scriptures say. We thus had to see it, as Isaiah and Revelation suggest. Then, we were there... among the hard, bleak, radical environments, the technicolor of an Everest, or just near a boulder in sun a simple day. The mountain is a way to show us what lies ahead and something that we were, before we were, and something of which we are capable and completely incapable. Light is a beautiful thing, when one ponders how many souls labor each day under some darkness of soul. In ice we find all that is nice and will suffice (forgive me Robert Frost), all the good tonnages of ice of Everest that say something to us of the weightlessness of our spirits.

There is no need for the drudgery of Everest. The experience is more powerful if we are light and, in a sense, immune to cold and to height. We skim through books about Everest late at night, to a point sometimes where blood begins to pool in our arms. We become expert on the subject of a mountain. It is amazing how many people speak authoritatively about Everest who never have, in the legal-material sense, climbed it. In this futuristic age of technical polish, it hardly behooves one to enter mountaineering in a first-hand way. John Krakauer's *Into Thin Air* always is there, if one wishes to read about what happens when one goes too aggressively at becoming the measure of a mountain. How is it that "Best Seller" should be printed on the cover of a book before the book appears on the store shelves?

We tend to buy books if we think they are best sellers, for we want to be in line with the mainstream. We want approval--even if vicarious. That also is why we climb Everest, or that is why some folks climb Everest. It is the thing to do. We will have aligned ourselves with the desire and fears of the masses. Only when Everest is not the thing to do will you ever convince me your climb was done for the right reasons. Would a publisher ever say, "Go back up there and do it right?" I don't remember what the subject of this chapter was, but I hope something that I have said will shed light on whatever the subject may have been. I suppose I wanted to speak about the mystery that adheres to starlight and mountain ridges—depending on perspective…, or that there are different ways in which to climb….

Often the reason for a visit to Everest must be to get away, to free oneself, to rise out of the road rage or suburban life, to keep from being swallowed by a mini-mall, or by a world that is work-a-day. The motivation for a climb, one as suicidal as Everest, may be to take a break from babies and a wife. Escape is key, undoubtedly, for climbers, but soon there follows a conscious recognition that the warm bed and a wife's warmth are better than the cold tent and no breath. She plays Scrabble, too. Strip Scrabble. You just have to spell the item of clothing.

Why attack a mountain? The punishment for such aggravated assault, no matter how good at climbing you are, is always at very least, and in the case of Everest, a little bit like humiliation or a wounded body. To go up onto these slopes and discipline yourself, your mind and flesh, by austerity and self-denial, to experience the ascetic discipline of suffering, the hypoxia, even in some cases to the point of becoming gangrenous or necrotic, to sit in a tent under circumstances of such claustrophobia and ice-hard thoughts and boredom, to struggle through wind in an attempt to hear the quiet mystery, perhaps to never hear or feel it… but rather to observe the slow approach of the end of the Neozoic Period, or the final groan of a torso wedged in ice, and to become aware that you will come home with six words of Indic language or, at best, a glint of Nepalese, along with, possibly, a trace of emotional disorder, or nervous exhaustion, that you will be incapacitated in some or other way, and that such an injury or condition, if only mental, will remain the focus of your being, and your control for the rest of your life will be hampered by an uneasiness, a subtle neurasthenia…. To be sure, you will have asked things of yourself. And you will be proud to have ventured up there to pay such a price. And you will realize also that lots of people are to be jealous of you and will hate you that you succeeded, or that you even partially succeeded, or they will despise you, as lots of people do, when you fall short in any way of a full, unquestionable success. An altogether different category of people will over-love you. Thus there is a point perhaps in finding inner and more silent ways.

I was moved by David Breashears' comment in his book about Goran Kropp's self-discipline and instinct, in turning back just below the summit. Breashears states, "It's never an easy decision to turn back. But such a decision greatly honors the mountain and yourself." (*High Exposure*, p. 250)

Darling, do you feel a draft?

10. WAIT UNTIL THE WIND IS RIGHT

"A cloud creates the face of a man who, happening to look up, recognizes it as his own. The face under stress of the wind begins to disintegrate into wings, and the man sees in himself the ability to fly. He stretches forth his arms and waves them up and down as he begins to circle and dip as a birdman would in the currents of the wind, and then the face vanishes and the wings drift apart, too, in shreds and patches."

—David Ignatow (*Whisper To The Earth*, p. 7)

Out of quiet…, a roar—an avalanche of wind. Chris Bonington writes in his diary, from his 1972 expedition, "The wind is the appalling enemy. It is mind-destroying, physically destroying, soul-destroying." (*Everest South West Face*, Chapter 12) Dougal Haston, commenting on the same expedition, said, "The wind—always the wind…. This was no silent journey up a crisp snowfield in the pure high air." (*Everest South West Face*, Chapter 16)

No one has spoken yet of a wind that blows upward against one's back, a wind that can be used to achieve the final 2000 feet to the summit. Imagine a wind that lifts, or pushes, instead of opposes. There must be opposition in all things, and we love challenge, yet there must also be ways to fashion our endeavors to the moment and adapt the weather to our ways, to acclimatize, calculate, and accommodate. Sounds like a song. The better mind will let the elements assist. If it rains, and one's car is dirty, a drive is called for, so that the rain may wash the car. If it is windy, you fly a kite... or you ride your bike with the wind against your back. There is a book yet to be written on how to build experience around wind. If the river is high, you don't wade it. If it is hot, the middle of July, you don't attempt a rock climb where holds will be slippery. On Everest, you don't go up the final strenuous section until the wind is aimed at your back from below.

The wind is one of those dynamics of the greatest of mountains. It hardly would be as frightening, or adventurous, could we predict the wind, could we turn the wind off and on. Yet somehow, I believe, there is a way for a climber, even on Everest, to keep from matching human fierceness and the fierceness of the wind.

Wind in most cases is a bad subject. There only are a few good things to say about wind. Everest would be an endless parade of idiots, tourists, etc. (more so than it is), but for the wind. In Boulder, Colorado, climbers have been blown off the final summit ridge of the Third Flatiron. Yet the warm, dry Chinook of the Rocky Mountains pushes smog away. On a hot day of climbing rock in Eldorado canyon, a breeze feels good. If you wind-surf or sail, wind is agreeable and necessary. There are nice memories that are associated with wind.

On Everest, so it has been said, the wind is unavoidable. It hangs on almost every moment and day of the action. If Everest is where we are to place our spirits, then we must accept the wind in its icy fury and not just wind, but a wind that goes mad. Of Everest weather, Tom Longstaff said, "Ten thousand devils are continually contending up there." (*Everest*, p. 134)

The elements in all their violence are what the big mountains are about, high wind slabs and storms that blow an unfortunate amount of your resolve away. Those who amble up Everest and, by some stroke, encounter no wind or weather are not blessed to know the strain to the psyche of an unabating wind. The test of Everest is not so much that it is a mountain but that it is wind. The test is for one to remain clear when the weather is not, to keep set on the goal, and sane, in the face of a squall that almost probably is not to let up. The Everest experience must include a few long, terrible nights in a tent torn and thrashed by wind. Such nights (or days) bring about a variety of moods, sometimes somber and lonely, sometimes ridiculous, people whispering, others in a delirious mumble, grandiose speculation amid weeping or jest. Levity alleviates laxity. Or is it that levity is a laxative? It is necessary to make light of despair, to joke, for there is no telling how close the mind might be to breaking.

Nice updraft, Menzel,
see you at Camp VI

Heinrich Harrer asks, "What climber worth his salt ever went crazy as a result of exertion, deadly peril or fear?" (*The White Spider*, p. 233) We fight to stay this side of the brink of whatever it is that wants to take us wherever we desire to go but from which we know we would never return.

Far up Everest, in a tent, Mallory and Somervell read Shakespeare to one another. Dialogue in a tent might be reduced in some moment to commentary about bodily functions. A small crudity is to be forgiven, deprived of oxygen as the Everest climber inevitably is. I will leave specifics of this sort for another journey and stray altogether away from the route of delving into the crisis of how men and women take showers or go to the bathroom on Everest. I will say only that one learns of Everest by processes of gale elimination.

I have small daydreams. Just now I had one that characterizes the absurdity of climbers. I see seven or eight climbers propelled around in the air on Everest, flying people with rockets strapped to their backs, who leave circular trails of smoke and laugh out of control, very round people… like balloons let go, and air shoots out of them like flatus….

We have deteriorated, as a result of exhaustion. We have come to the end of our little romp of Everest. I have walked with you down--and safely I will note. We are at the bottom of the mountain…. I will confess that I switched a thermos of hot drink, from your pack to mine, when you were not looking. This was to keep you from yourselves, to keep such provisions from being consumed before you had earned them. It is important to stay at a level of suffering, if we are to take home the adventure, if we are to have something to savor, if we are to be Henry the V's "few, we happy few." (*King Henry V*, Act IV, Scene III) You will be restored soon to the soft and good aspects of life, but there will exist interiors of your life that never were there before.

Though the summit was reached without tragedy, and no part of the mountain collapsed on us, I am gratified to be down (as I am sure you are). I am indebted to the gods of the mountain, that I stand now at the place which happens, by fate, also to be two or three pages from the end of this book. I am out of breath, out of gas... as it were. I have another confession. The person who has been talking to you all this time has not been Pat Ament. It has been George Leigh-Mallory. I have been your companion. I have used Ament's body as my vehicle, my disguise.

I wish to compliment you for your achievement, in climbing Everest. You have ventured up onto the mountain. I had only to talk you through, in places. And you heard me. You have been transfigured, although you may not know it. Your face is crowned with radiance. You have a special, heavenward shiver. And while I have played with words and made light of things that are serious to some, I am more serious than I seem. You will feel my respect, if you dig with a snow shovel between the lines, if you circumvent the firmament, for a moment, with your thoughts. Did Irvine and I make it to the summit in 1924?

I will offer a poem of Shakespeare's, one that Somervell...and later my friend Irvine... enjoyed when I read it to them in a tent. It is a love poem, perhaps. I do not suggest the poem's words were said with an intent for any companion of mine, yet I did and do love them. I find in the lines, rather, application to this, Sir George Everest the surveyor's, mountain, Chomolungma:

> Shall I compare thee to a summer's day?
> Thou art more lovely and more temperate:
> Rough winds do shake the darling buds of May,
> And summer's lease hath all too short a date:
> Sometime too hot the eye of heaven shines,
> And often is his gold complexion dimmed;

And every fair from fair sometime declines,
By chance or nature's changing course untrimmed;
But thy eternal summer shall not fade,
Nor lose possession of that fair thou owest;
Nor shall Death brag thou wander'st in his shade,
When in eternal lines to time thou growest:
  So long as men can breathe, or eyes can see,
  So long lives this, and this gives life to thee.
(Sonnet 18)

Everest jolts us with a power—one that is in part an exultation we feel at having been to these realms with each other, as friends, our small colony of artists rich in the poverty of our spirits, pathologically shy, full of love and sin, wild with reverence and hope, half mystics, half hermits. Our minds are on the sculpture. We see it, a mountain that is here perhaps for no other reason than to convey to us the effect, the countenance, of luminous space. We look back at Everest, a moment as though we suddenly are able to remember something sacred and beautiful from some far away past. There is a numbness to our fingers, and there is pain in our optic nerves—the sharp consequence of our rise for a time above normally more synthetic vision. Everest unfolds things to us, as it destroys the architecture of its own body. Hidden in and under the mountain, and all around it, is a mystical, linear elegance, an atmosphere, the long, jewel-like ridges. There is a meaning for us, an extended journey, a project of inspiration to which our minds always will be apprenticed.

The mountains are an exultant image whose mirrors create the effect of endlessly receding planes. Their image is suddenly clear, then is blurred, an expression of our presence. Then we are gone. We were never known. Everest does not attract attention to itself. It obscures itself among other mountains, finds secrecy in its weather and moods. Yet it preserves the integrity of its silhouettes. A cold ghostliness speaks of anguished figures. There is a strangeness, one of a beautiful worth. A storm breaks. We are called to its prismatic, poetic mood, a beauty that pervades every part of us… like a sorrow… for all that is given, and that we are blessed to know, …and must leave hidden.

Clootie, you look
just like my knees

So this is it?

Time for a fresh oxygen cylinder

REVIEW

1. Realize it's just not an important thing to do.
2. Bring lots of ladders.
3. Have yaks and Sherpas carry all the heavy stuff.
4. Realize far worse climbers than you have done it.
5. Realize far better climbers than you have failed at it.
6. Realize you have already succeeded at harder climbs.
7. Realize you have already failed at easier climbs.
8. Realize you will never be as good as Hermann Buhl, and he never did Everest.
9. Realize there are more ways than one to climb Everest.
10. Wait until the wind is right.

BIBLIOGRAPHY

Bonatti, Walter, *The Great Days*. Translated by Geoffrey Sutton, Victor Gollancz, Ltd., London, 1976

Bonington, Chris, *The Everest Years*, A Climber's Life. Viking, 1987

Breashears, David, *High Exposure*. Simon & Shuster, 1999

Broughton, Coburn, Edited by, *Everest, Mountain Without Mercy*. National Geographic Society, ©MacGillivray Freeman Films, 1997

Brown, Joe, *The Hard Years*. Penguin Books, England, 1975 (first published by Victor Gollancz, 1967)

Craig, David, *Landmarks*. Jonathan Cape (Random House), United Kingdom, 1995

Desmaison, Rene, *Total Alpinism*. Translated by Jane Taylor, Granada Publishing, 1982

Diemberger, Kurt, *Summits and Secrets*. the Mountaineers, Seattle, 1991 (original English translation published in Great Britain, by Grafton, 1971)

Harrer, Heinrich, *The White Spider*. Hart-Davis, MacGibbon, London, 1959

Hornbein, Tom, *Everest, the West Ridge* (abridged). The Sierra Club, Ballantine Books, California, 1968

Howard-Bury, Lt. Col. C. K. (and others), *Mount Everest: the Reconnaissance*. Edward Arnold & Co., London, 1921

Ignatow, David, *Whisper To The Earth*. Little, Brown and Company, Boston, 1981

Messner, Reinhold, *Free Spirit*. Translated by Jill Neate, the Mountaineers, Seattle, 1991

Nemerov, Howard, *Figures of Thought*. David R. Godine, Publisher, Inc., 1978

Noel, Captain John, *The Story of Everest*. Little, Brown, & Co., Boston, 1927

Norton, Lt. Col. E. F., *The Fight for Everest*. Edward Arnold & Co., London, 1924

Robbins, Royal, *Advanced Rockcraft*. La Siesta Press, California, 1973

Robinson, Doug, *A Night on the Ground, a Day in the Open*. Mountain N' Air Books, California, 1996

Saner, Reg, *Reaching Keet Seel*. University of Utah Press, Salt Lake City, 1998

Scott, Doug, *Himalayan Climber*. Baton Wicks, London, 1992

Smith, George Alan and Carol D., Edited by, *The Armchair Mountaineer*. Pitman Publishing Corp., New York, 1968

Somervell, T. Howard, *After Everest*. Hodder & Stoughton, London, 1936

Terray, Lionel, *Conquistadors of the Useless*. Translated by Geoffrey Sutton, Victor Gollancz, Ltd., London, 1963

Ullman, James Ramsey, *Kingdom of Adventure*. William Sloane Associates, Inc., New York, 1947

Unsworth, Walt, *Everest*. Grafton (HarperCollins Publishers), London, 1989

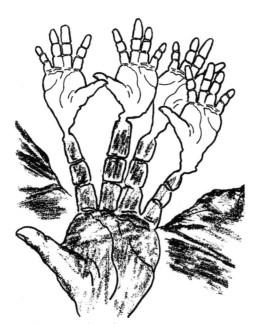

Finger check